FAREWELL
MY LORDS

For Franklin

fr Ad Mitchell

Farewell
My Lords

By
Austin Mitchell

First published in Great Britain 1999
by Politico's Publishing
8 Artillery Row
London
SW1P 1RZ
United Kingdom
Tel 0171 931 0090
Email politicos@artillery-row.demon.co.uk
Website http://www.politicos.co.uk

A catalogue record of this book is available from the British Library

ISBN 1902301439

Printed and bound in Great Britain by St. Edmundsbury Press
Typesetting by John Berry for Politico's Publishing
Cover Design By Ad Vantage

Austin Mitchell is the MP for
Great Grimsby. His previous books
include *Westminster Man,*
Last Time: Labour's Lessons From the Sixties,
The Case for Labour and
Four Years in the Death of the Labour Party

CONTENTS

A Walk Down the Corridor

THIS is an oral portrait of the House of Lords as described by its members in their own words. I talked on tape to nearly 50 peers, a twentieth of the membership: hereditary and life peers, of all parties and none, and a wide range of ages. All gave willingly of their time and opinions. The result is a picture of the House, the tribe who inhabit it, their work and life as they themselves see it: a practical sociology of the Peer People at a crucial time in their half-lives.

They're an endearing lot, working mostly part-time in a quaint and uniquely British institution, at a traditional job they do out of duty, and certainly not for reward, and revelling in it. They're gratified by interest from outside, easily hurt, anxious about what's to come but all perfectly ready, even eager, to talk about their work, their role, themselves and the kind of second chamber they'd like to see. Interviewing started just before the 1997 election and ended in December 1998. As it went on, the charm, anxieties and concerns and the overwhelming niceness of the peers I talked to ensured that I became increasingly sympathetic to a life form and an institution I'd previously regarded with amused indifference while taking very little interest in it, despite being a neighbour of 20 years standing.

Cries of "Coming to join us?" and "Looking over the place ready for your retirement?" greeted me on some of my trips down the corridor to meet the more likeable, better bred and less obviously pushy and ambitious breed of parliamentarians at the other end. Some even invited me to their stately homes until I pointed out that they were the class enemy of New Labour - the only one. They're so much nicer, more subdued and easier to get on with than the careerists who trample over each other at the green carpeted end where MPs are so much nearer the centre of power, so much further from the real world. They're pleased when people take an interest in them, unlike the Commons who resent it when people don't. They're all amazingly diffident: when I asked one if I could take off my jacket in the tea room he nervously asked the waiter - who resentfully pointed out that some were wearing roll-neck sweaters so anything goes! To go the 100 yards along that corridor is to go back a 100 years in terms of courtesy, a sensibly relaxed approach to politics and the processes and rules of debates. They've got the day-to-day politics, which obsess MPs, in proper perspective as necessary interludes between chats with friends.

So 'thank you' to all the peers who gave so willingly of their time and views. This is their book, though I've arranged, abridged and edited their contributions, which are reproduced here with all the qualifications, repetitions and er-um-ulps that political flesh is heir to (and aristocracy more than most) all taken out to produce a coherent text. I hope this does what I set out to achieve by showing the living reality of an institution peripheral to power politics but now central to the political and constitutional debate, not just for the coming year of the initial reform, but for far longer. The announcement of reform in the 1998 Queen's Speech should and will open up a prolonged debate and the prospect of further reform (which will be necessary, but not necessarily forthcoming) for a long time beyond that. The peers are the last people to have been consulted in all this. So this is their opportunity to tell us what the victims think and feel: the highest focus group in the land and the only one with a direct interest in its own fate.

I did the interviewing, except for half a dozen peers who were interviewed by my wife for her programme "Westminster Women"; Tim Grewal organised everything, kept the project moving forward and did the research, along with Tony Field, a parliamentary intern from the University of Hull. Pat Murray, Dawne Seaton and Joyce Benton prepared the text and coped with the endless changes. I'm grateful to all of them.

AUSTIN MITCHELL

LORDS INTERVIEWED

The Viscount Allenby of Megiddo	Hereditary, Cross-Bencher
The Lord Bruce of Donington	Labour
The Lord Colwyn, CBE	Hereditary, Conservative
The Rt. Hon. the Viscount Cranborne, DL	Hereditary, Conservative
The Lord Dahrendorf, KBE, FBA	Liberal Democrat
The Rt. Hon. The Lord Denham, KBE	Hereditary, Conservative
The Duke of Devonshire, KG, PC, MC	Hereditary, Cross-Bencher
The Lord Donoughue	Labour
The Lord Dubs	Labour
The Viscount of Falkland	Hereditary, Liberal Democrat
The Earl of Glasgow, DL	Hereditary, Liberal Democrat
The Lord Graham of Edmonton	Labour
The Lord Harmer-Nicholls	Conservative
The Rt. Hon. the Lord Healey, CH, MBE	Labour
The Lord Henley	Hereditary, Conservative
The Lord Hollick	Labour
The Baroness Hollis of Heigham, DL	Labour
The Lord Inglewood, ARICS, DL	Hereditary, Conservative
The Lord Kennet	Hereditary, Labour
The Bishop of Lincoln	N/A
The Rt. Hon. The Earl of Longford, KG	Hereditary, Labour
The Lord McCarthy	Labour
The Lord Mcintosh of Haringey	Labour
The Countess of Mar	Hereditary, Cross-Bencher
The Lord McNally	Liberal Democrat
The Lord Monkswell	Hereditary, Labour
The Earl of Onslow	Hereditary, Conservative
The Baroness O'Cathain, OBE	Conservative
The Lord Putnam, CBE	Labour
The Lord Ponsonby of Shulbrede	Hereditary, Labour
The Rt. Hon. the Lord Renton, KBE, QC, TD, DL	Conservative
The Lord Redesdale	Hereditary, Liberal Democrat
The Rt Hon, the Lord Richard QC	Labour
Professor the Earl Russell, FBA	Hereditary, Liberal Democrat
The Lord Stoddart of Swindon	Labour
The Baroness Strange	Hereditary, Conservative
The Lord Strabolgi	Hereditary, Labour
The Rt. Hon. the Lord of Strathclyde	Hereditary, Conservative
The Lord Sudeley	Hereditary, Conservative
The Lord Taylor of Warwick	Conservative
The Lord Tordoff	Liberal Democrat
The Rt. Hon. the Baroness Trumpington of Sandwich, PC	Conservative
The Lord Wallace of Saltaire	Liberal Democrat
The Baroness Wharton	Hereditary, Cross-Bencher
The Lord Whitty	Labour
The Rt. Hon. the Lord Weatherill, DL	Cross-Bencher
The Rt. Hon. the Baroness Young, DL	Conservative

CHAPTER ONE

About the House

THE House of Lords is a quaint British institution. The quaintest in a country which turns quaintness into a system of government, as well as being the home of the quaintest officers, rituals and myths. The Lords do nothing in particular but do it very well. Certainly much to the satisfaction of the members, known in this world of Peers -R-Us as "lifers" and "hereds". Variously described as the British Senate, the geriatric ward of the constitution, God's Waiting Room, Mr Balfour's (now William Hague's) poodle, the Sunset Home for elderly politicians, or the Aldermanic Bench of politics, the Lords manages to be both the best and the worst part of the "mother of parliaments".

The best because it contains expertise, wisdom and experience which the Commons could never aspire to. Its debates are serious, often wiser and better-informed than the play-way party politics of the lower chamber. Yet also the worst because membership ranges from the sage to the batty, the perennial attender to the rare visitor. Its members can be irrelevant, even silly and prejudiced, and because there is little logical justification for its existence in its present form and none for the built-in Tory majority. Few were particularly concerned about the issue before Labour took it up. But there is nothing to explain why the majority of its members - the hereditary peers - should have the right to be in Parliament just because they inherited titles, and often wealth, from forebears who were monastic land grabbers, Charles II's pimps, greedy oligarchs during the long Whig hegemony of the 18th century or peerage purchasers in Lloyd George's discount sale.

The best and the worst are inseparable. The lack of a logical basis for membership other than past or present patronage makes them a motley flock whose lack of a legitimate base makes it difficult for the Lords to assert powers, check the elective dictatorship, take firm stands based on principle, or even find a useful role. Once there was no question of their authority. The Lords were the first chamber in power and status terms because up to the 19th century an aristocratic oligarchy effectively ruled, and largely owned, Britain. Prime Ministers regularly sat in the Lords right up to the time of the great Marquess of Salisbury who, from 1895 to 1903, ruled from there as Prime Minister into the present century.

Mass democracy and the rise of party changed all that and turned the Lords into a backwater. National parties linked organised parties in Parliament with mass membership in the country, enabling the people to choose the government. The party winning a majority in the country became all powerful. The ruling party expressed the popular will, and held the popular mandate. So, in this system of government by party, the power of the Lords declined as did its power base in a mass democracy built on universal suffrage. Through the majority party the executive controlled the legislature, which was the Commons, who became dominant, the Lords less relevant, less important and less controlled.

Property, wealth, and peers who had both, had long feared that the extension of the franchise would make political equality the first step to social equality, because it was assumed that the people would use political power to redistribute wealth even, in the worst of noble nightmares, to expropriate it. Eventually, though belatedly, this process did indeed begin in the Asquith Liberal Government before the First World War. The Lords resisted even this mild Liberal vision and, in doing so, lost their most important power: to say "no" to financial bills. Others they could delay only for two years, reduced to one by Labour, the next redistributive government, in 1949.

Since then the Lords have taken a back seat. Red pile plush to match their own ermine trim but still subordinate. Because, less important, they have remained amateurs in a political system which is becoming increasingly professional. Once the Commons had been amateurs, an assembly of gentlemen, many of them related to the aristocratic elite, some sitting for seats controlled by peers. In the 20th century new men, new classes and new issues centred around redistribution thrust their way onto the political scene. So aristocratic power declined and career politics - full time, professional and dedicated to the pursuit of power individually and collectively, rather than public service - became the dominant pattern.

By the 1990s the Commons were more youthful, well-paid, backed by professional staff and largely subordinate to the parties. The Lords were older with the average age of the life peers being 71. Although they were paid, but far from well, they were unstaffed, with few offices, and most members attending as irregularly as they chose. Like an amateur club left lingering in the third division and overawed by the premier league, they were an amateur assembly doing their duty part-time, all for very little money. The hereditaries are, on the whole, people of substantial wealth. 60% of them are landowners and farmers, ranging up to the Duke of Buccleuch, the largest private landowner in Britain with £400 million of land and property in Scotland. Two-fifths have had careers in the forces and three-quarters of the Tory hereditaries had been educated at one of the top seven public schools.

This made them very unrepresentative but, at the same time, the cheapest major parliamentary assembly in the world . Pay peanuts, get peers. Indeed this is now advanced as an argument against the change to professionalisation and a properly paid membership, rather than an assembly exploiting the good will of prominent people. The sense of duty of hereditaries would, and should, cost far more. Pathetic pay for peers can only be sustained as long as the Lords remains a part-time, amateur body, exploiting the goodwill of its members. Professionalise it, and proper pay becomes essential.

The strength of the Lords is its weakness. With no power they have been no threat, and hardly worth doing anything about. Because party was weaker in the Lords, the members became more respected than the party dominated Commons. They were freer and more independent in a way the nervous English middle classes liked, particularly when the institution spoke in the kind of accent they could defer to. Without a legitimate basis they were less assertive and less of a nuisance. When they challenged government it was in a mild, almost deferential, and easily overruled way: a nuisance not a negation, an inconvenience not an inhibition. The lords weren't even strong enough to provoke a Labour government into doing anything about the soft obstacle in its way. Harold Wilson attempted reform in the 60s but quickly desisted when the process proved messy, divisive and time-consuming.

The preamble to the 1911 Parliament Act boldly declared the intention "to substitute for the House of Lords as presently constituted a second chamber constituted on a popular instead of a hereditary basis". Nothing happened until right at the end of the century because it was easier to let sleeping peers lie and accept their low level usefulness while ignoring the issue of replacement or reform because it lacked urgency, whatever radicals might say or however much militants, ever attracted to symbolic rather than real issues, might rant. Little serious was proposed and even less was done. The Lords sat on unchallenged and unchanged, safe in the strength of their own weaknesses. There was no consensus on what to do about them and, with no agreement on an alternative, the subject became difficult and deferable; a playground for perfectionists, constitutionalists, obsessives and others of the same ilk: anoraks without ermine linings. Rien ne dure comme la maison des Lords. Far easier to tinker, as the Tory Acts of 1958 and 1963 did, by introducing life peerages to give it a new life, and entitling all Scottish peers (who had formerly elected some of their number) and peeresses to sit.

Now some, though very few, urge abolition. In fact, unicameralism as a strategy is difficult because the workload of modern legislatures - particularly the British - is such that an overworked Commons could not manage without a second chamber to ease its burden. Yet if there had to be a second chamber what was it to be? Elective? In which case it would challenge the Commons, particularly if, as some proposed, it was elected by proportional representation - a fairer system than first past the post which gives absolute power to governments elected on a minority vote. Yet the alternative, a nominated chamber would be an echo-chamber to the party in power, responding to its imperatives, dancing to its tune and obeying the executive authority which created it rather than checking it. Indeed it would strengthen the executive. Patronage is a major power, and a wholly nominated second chamber could be the greatest patronage quango ever, anywhere. Without the firm foundation of a federal constitution, a compromise between the two positions in the form perhaps of a chamber of regions, of interests or excellence, or any mix bringing together some nominated and some elective members, could only be built on marshy ground and might combine the disadvantages of both.

Such tensions have inhibited every attempt at reform. Safer to keep the status quo. There have been intermittent proposals for reform but none have commanded widespread support and none have been successful. For practical purposes there has been no clear, generally accepted, alternative to the House of Lords, a difficulty demonstrated by Labour's 1968 reform. Accepted by the peers and introduced by a government with a majority of 100, this was killed by an unholy alliance of Enoch Powell, who wanted a more powerful hereditary chamber, and Michael Foot who wanted the Lords abolished. On that deadlock the Bill foundered in the face of a fillibuster and Harold Wilson threw in the ermine towel.

Thus the Lords carried on for decades, reform always possible but never happening, just one of those perennial, abstract and unimportant questions with which the irrational British constitution is festooned. Unjustifiable and little justified, but working well at a limited, low key, but useful role and not frustrating any government enough to provoke action. The Lords have been an oubliette in the constitutional 'file and forget'cupboard which is full of things which might - indeed should - be done someday, but probably won't happen because other problems are always, rightly, more urgent. Why bother?

Until the 90s. Then Labour, for no very clear reason, took up the issue, not of abolition which it had wanted in the early 80s, but had forgotten along with so many of the other things it had wanted at that time, but abolition of the hereditary majority. Inheriting a seat in Parliament is illogical and happens nowhere else, though Nigeria once had its House of Chiefs. Abolition looked straightforward: cheap easy, quick and unlikely to arouse protest, apart from some of the hereditary peers themselves. It was something to do and it conferred on an increasingly moderate, even conservative, New Labour Party the radical edge which so many of its rank and file found lacking. It also faced up to a problem which had always haunted Labour: the possibility of power without any real majority. Moreover, it did all this without upsetting business, the media, or middle England in the way public ownership, redistribution or real radicalism would have done. It also fitted in with the Government's constitutional strategy of distributing power down to the people. Or rather, would do if reform went beyond the abolition of hereditary peers. Finally, it tied in well with the other major strand of New Labour thinking: modernisation. What could be more modern than to scrap hereditary privilege, and what could be easier than to modernise by mugging the easiest victim in the country, one very few would or could defend? This was the kind of fight New Labour liked.

Labour, committed by its manifesto, is now acting on its undertaking, though how and whether it will go beyond abolition of hereditary peers into a stage two, which was envisaged but remains more difficult and still undefined, still remains unclear. What is clear is that the lords themselves will not play any real part in shaping their own fate unless they up the ante by bitter resistance in the hope of forcing the Government to the negotiating table, an unlikely development when the Government itself can opt for divide and rule, dangling the prospect of some peers sitting on before their Lordships.

Hence this portrait of the peers by their peers. In it they describe in their own words how the House of Lords works, its strengths and weaknesses. This paints a picture of the House before modernisation, showing the peers, their role and their preoccupations as the peers themselves see them. It isn't so much an oral history, not even a verbal obituary, but the peers' own picture of their institution and their job, with only minimal flavouring and colouring added. Not Moriamus te Salutamus , but they (or at least some of them) who are about to fade into history, salute themselves.

IT'S very easy to point out what's wrong with the House of Lords, and nobody can defend the hereditary system which is completely indefensible by any standards. But when you begin to consider what you want to put in its place, you come across greater problems. I think the best defence of the House of Lords is that it is something that has grown up organically, historically, and it works in practice but not in theory. But it doesn't quite work in practice and the main area is the inbuilt number of Conservative hereditary peers, which is obviously completely indefensible. It's a farce in many ways.

The Earl of Glasgow, Liberal Democrat

You are always impressed by the House of Lords if you know nothing about the subject. They put on a magnificent show but talk more unmitigated rubbish about any subject than you ever saw in your life. The more you know about the subject the less you respect them. If you don't know about the subject it's absolutely first class stuff. We have the king of it, Lord Jenkins, who could talk about anything while knowing nothing about anything. These people are very good at performing. If you know what's going on you're not so impressed.

Lord McCarthy, Labour

It is an organic House. There is a texture to it. You can tell the mood when you go in each day at Question Time, you know how it's going to go, whether it's going to be tipped over into surliness, into being obstreperous, or whether it's going to be generous and supportive, tired and bored. There is a temperature you can pick up there. All of that organic thing is being diluted by a lot of extra new peers on both sides who we haven't gauged yet or haven't properly come into the system. But it is a live animal.

Lady Hollis, Labour

It's kind of like an old people's club. Well, you don't notice that people are so terribly old. It's only when you come up from the other place and you look in the House and you say, "God, is he still alive?".

Lord Tordoff, Liberal Democrat

The Gilbert and Sullivan touch is obviously the major, immediate impact. The role, the emphasis, the ludicrous introduction ceremony. Partly because

10

there's a certain courtliness about the whole thing. There is a lot of underlying conflict in the House of Lords but it's dealt with in a sort of courteous, chivalrous manner. Not quite all the time. Sometimes it gets bitter but most of the time it is like medieval rituals of courtesy which you don't find in other walks of life any more. That actually is quite seductive but we shouldn't take it too seriously. It's not a proper decision-making body for the modern age. The age since about 1650.

Lord Whitty, Labour

Those who were there before life peers say that it's become much more lively with life peers, because it's brought in a lot of people, very distinguished people, from all walks of life who, if they don't come all the time, come to contribute on issues about which they know a very great deal. I think they have a profound effect on government ministers. There is nothing more alarming, when you're getting up to reply at the dispatch box, and somebody opposite you says, "Would the minister consider her brief? I have lived in this country in Central Africa for the last 25 years and I'm not quite sure that she's right." So at once you're not only in trouble, you're in great trouble and it's that kind of thing in the House. You never quite know when you're going to get it.

Lady Young, Conservative

What should an octogenarian widower do to keep himself out of mischief except tender advice and make a measured contribution? I've had a very varied life in peace and war. I served in the army all through the war, had a good practise at the Bar, had some judicial experience. I was in the government for seven years. So people seem to think I've got something to contribute, and I do. I make fairly frequent speeches. I do come most days.

Lord Renton, Conservative

I think it is a paradox that the Senior House is in fact the Junior House. The second chamber is there in a revisory and an advisory role, but it brings a certain independence from the whips and it does enable independent minds to question the executive. Question Time in the Lords is quite an impressive occasion. It's different. I always think that the Lords is playing spin bowling and the Commons is playing fast bowling. You don't get the bouncers whistling round your head in the Lords, and both asking questions and making a speech is entirely different. The first thing you've got to get used to is the respectful silence in which you're heard, whereas in the Commons you can actually play off the noise to a certain extent. That's extremely unnerving at first. The realisation that you've got ten minutes and that they are going to listen to you is quite unnerving.

Lord McNally, Liberal Democrat

It has changed and everybody's trying to change things. Unnecessarily. We may be a dinasour but we're a living dinasour. We give an enormous amount of pleasure and interest to peole all over the country. It's amazing how many people, strangers, write to me and a) ask for help and b) express their opinion. Sometimes they just write mad letters. Anyway, I get the damnedest letters you've ever seen. Quite a lot from prisoners.

Lady Trumpington, Conservative

People coming up from the Commons get very impatient. They want to know why they simply can't exercise muscle and discipline. That's not where we find ourselves. This is an 18th century House. You put together alliances on particular issues. There are particular lobbies. For example, there's a very powerful Green lobby who really know about the environment in this place, and that goes across all parties. There's a very powerful disability lobby which runs across from Brian Rix on the crossbenches and people on the Tory benches to people on our side like Jack Ashley and Alf Morris. Virtually every charity in the country, their patron or their president sits here because they're all peers of the realm or Lord Lieutenants. That means that when a big issues comes up in the Commons which would be regarded as somehow soggy, or women's issues, here it's central. They speak to it and they're briefed by their organisations. Providing you work the pressure group organ-isations you can use them to exert leverage and get cross-benchers to come in behind you.

Lady Hollis, Labour

I'm the only person in the UK who has served 15 years as the head of a local authority, 25 years in the House of Commons, 20 years in the House of Lords, and 5 years in the European Parliament. Of all of them the most effective and the one that in my view is the most valuable up to the level of its powers is the House of Lords. Without any question. Because it's made up of all the elements. It's made up of the cross-benchers, people who've been brought in because of their professional or academic standing, the hereditary peers who ensure that you've got an incursion of young people because the hereditary peers bring the young ones and they are very good. Some of them are useless but by and large they are very good.

Lord Harmar-Nicholls, Conservative

I rate the quality of debates in the Lords much higher than in the Commons. When I go and sit in the Commons (and I do quite often) the quality of speech now is nothing like it used to be. I really think that I could take a number of my own people on my own side and a number of backbenchers from the Tory side, and I could interchange them because they are there for a career rather than for a conviction. In the Lords there is more time to reflect and to study. Against that you have the onset of age which makes them less capable by the sheer action of time to devote detailed study, but by and large they do have more time to reflect and more time to prepare.

Lord Bruce, Labour

The history is one of continuity rather than change. The principle adaptation happened in the Attlee Government with the enormous Labour majority in the House of Commons and an enormous overall Conservative majority in the House of Lords. They had to work out some modus vivendi and Salisbury and Addison, the two leaders, got together and worked out the Salisbury-Addison convention whereby basically you'd not kill a bill at second reading or even by wrecking amendment at committee. So the House became a revising chamber. Because they were giving up their right to take decisions on fundamental matters they've always been given more freedom by their parties in voting on smaller matters and to that extent there has always been much more of a cross-party feeling. One has friends on all sides and outside the Chamber, there's no difference between the parties.

Lord Denham, Conservative

It isn't an old gentleman's club. First of all, there are 95, nearly 100 women here now. So it isn't all gentlemen. I don't know what a gentlemen's club is anyway, never having been a member but a gentlemen's club is like this place where you meet very interesting people, where you can debate issues as wide-ranging as the Civil War in the States. You actually have a level of respect for people, and every person is respected by everybody else. There are no sort of snide comments or backstabbing that you get in practically every other walk of life. Who wants rivals? There's enough rivalry in the world, there's enough competitiveness in the business world without having competition and rivals here.

Lady O'Cathain, Conservative

The century began with a Cecil as Prime Minister in the Lords, and it's almost coming to an end with a Cecil as Leader of the Lords. I hope what will happen is a look at how you can keep some of the elements of the Lords that are undoubtedly a success: the cross-benchers and their role; the role of the select committees in the Lords; the opportunity to have slightly broader based debates that the Lords have on a variety of subjects, which the Commons just never gets round to doing. I think you've got to leave the power and the political pace-making in the Commons, but keep the Lords ability to revise, advise, and to take these broader strategic looks at policy, and to bring in expertise which the Commons doesn't necessarily bring into the system.

Lord McNally, Liberal Democrat

It is the most beautiful chamber, and you have a great sense of history sitting in there and people behave very properly. It's not a zoo like the House of Commons. You don't have retarded teenagers shouting silly things at one another, and laughing at the most appalling jokes. People conduct themselves well, it's self-regulated, there's no Speaker, but there's understood rules and conventions. I found it quite impressive.

Lord Donoughue, Labour

The greatest thing I think one can do in this chamber is we can embarrass the Government. I think Question Time in the Lords is one of the more useful elements. I asked one of the Lords ministers the other week and she said, "Tell me why you put down this question?" And I said, "I just wanted to know whether you're all on auto-pilot from the last government or whether you've actually thought through this one", and she said, "Well actually, I read the file last night and I think you're right, we are on auto-pilot." So you gain at least by making the ministers read through files to reconsider what they're doing. If one's content to recognise that second order elements in politics are useful, then being in the Lords is. Bits of it, I enjoy immensely. There are some debates which are pure joy, in which everyone who gets up is expert. The opposite extreme, the other week, there was a debate on the importance of Territorial Army and Reserve Forces in the light of the current Defence Review. It was the Lords' worst. A selection of retired Generals, Air Marshalls, Scots Guardsmen, whatever else, were reminiscing about their time in the Army fifty years ago. It wasted five hours of my time. So it's very mixed. Parts of it, I enjoy immensely. Other parts, I would miss out.

Lord Wallace, Liberal Democrat

When I first came here they had a bill on agricultural tenancies and I didn't know anything about agricultural tenancies, but there were people here who knew all about them because they'd got them at the bottom of their estates. Or when they had the Deer Bill or the Salmon Bill, there are people who know and they know because basically they own the deer and the salmon. So there was a whole world which I hadn't got any sense of. Some of the people are very odd. They are not the sort of ordinary run-of-the-mill people that one normally meets. If you want to have tea there's a peers dining room, and you sit at a very long table. I'm very careful about going in there with friends because you could be sitting in there next to anybody and they have the most bizarre views on life. They have views which are not in the real world and you're stuck there for the whole lunch or tea. So you've got to be very careful who you sit next to.

Lord Dubs, Labour

I think that if members of the House of Commons would really work full time and do nothing else you wouldn't need a second chamber. But they won't. So we do. Anyway, legislation comes in such a dogs' breakfast way, and half the time the civil servants don't know what they're doing, and the parliamentary draftsman doesn't know what he's doing. You have to have a period of time in which things can be improved, drafting can be improved, and this House of Lords might as well do it.

Lord McCarthy, Labour

There's no arrangement which is both effective and logical. The hereditary system has done a good job here in a lot of ways but it does produce a gross party imbalance. It can't go on, simply because one can't stand up and defend it. I remember my wife saying to me once, "Can you give me one good reason why it should be you and not me?" I tried to answer it once and I haven't made the same mistake twice. Reform depends entirely on how clear we are about stage two. I don't think it will be acceptable if we're simply asked to accept a fully-appointed chamber. If I were here as an appointed peer and not as a hereditary peer, I wouldn't feel any more legitimate as a result. As a hereditary, I feel as if I'm here as the result of a rigged lottery. As an appointed peer, I would feel that I was here because of having appeal to my party leader. If I was excluded I would mind desperately, but I wouldn't really feel I could shout about it unless I were convinced the successor arrangement was inadequate. Then I would feel I could shout about it.

Because we have hitherto thought we were together 'til death do us part, we do all learn to accept each other. That loyalty to each other is something really admirable. I don't know whether that will survive reform. I'll be very, very sad if it doesn't. It goes with the principle which was established in Cromwell's day, that all peers count equal. This degree of acceptance of each other, the friendships across the party and all the rest, those are really vital.

Lord Russell, Liberal Democrat

Because the House of Lords is so precarious, it is not sure of its position in a democratic society. It has to tread extremely carefully in what it can do and, therefore, it doesn't even dare use the powers that it actually has got.

Earl of Glasgow, Liberal Democrat

There is no power here except that we're an advising chamber and we amend legislation on that basis. I think the two key respects in which the situation is much worse than in the Commons is that I don't have a sense of legitimacy. When I was MP for Battersea I had the legitimacy of knowing that I represented people. I don't have that now and hereditary peers wouldn't understand that because they believe they have a sense of legitimacy for other reasons, such as 20 generations of whatever it is. So this lack of legitimacy makes me say to myself, "Well who am I to have an opinion". OK, I'm the same guy who was down the other end of the building and I hope in the same way that I go along with the bulk of Labour Party policy and so on, but I still have doubts as to how much entitlement I have to put my opinions forward, though it doesn't stop me. The other thing is not having a constituency.

Lord Dubs, Labour

I would press for an elected second chamber because I think if you're going to have a truly representative chamber it should be an elected chamber. There is a full-time role here. One of the great dangers is how you manage to combine people who've got particular experience in one section and probably have a continuing involvement there, with a full-time job. I think the workload here is not so great as to completely exclude continuing to work as a teacher or a doctor or a journalist. An elected chamber would give a better representation, a balance, and more authority. There are occasionally debates in the House of Lords which are very satisfying to those who take part in them but have absolutely no effect outside, and that's a bit depressing. A club speaking to itself. But there are other occasions where the House of Lords made an impact on government, as its meant to. Where does government listen? Well, I don't know. Do governments listen? You can't tell when your are listened to and who listens. Having been on the other side I know how selective one's perception is of what's being said. I have no great illusions about it. So the simple answer is, occasionally, yes.

Lord Dahrendorf, Liberal Democrat

All I would say is, it's a great life. One of the sadnesses is of course there are colleagues all round you - Peter Thornicroft is a good case - when I came up in '83, he was hail and hearty. You then see him needing a stick, then having to use a wheelchair. Then fade away. You actually see the deterioration. In some cases, you see them not well, and in some cases, you don't see them again until they die. I used to say to myself, "Why on earth is this man or woman bothering to come here to parade the fact that they're not well?" The sad fact is that if many of them didn't come here, they would die. So, I say good luck to them. I haven't got a stick or wheelchair yet, but I've got my name down for them.

Lord Graham, Labour

CHAPTER TWO

Peers-R-Us

LIKE the Palace of Westminster, the Lords deceive to impress. The Palace is a venerable Gothic facade to conceal a legislative factory. The lords look like a repository of history and tradition, with historic titles handed down over long generations into the mists of time, but aren't as antique as they act. The title of the Countess of Mar, Premier Earl of Scotland (who lives and farms in Surrey), is claimed to go back to 1114 though it is only provable to 1404. The other oldest titles held by members of the Lords are De Ros (1264), Mobray and Stourton (1283), Hastings (1290), and Clinton (1299), while the title of Lord Strabolgi, a Labour hereditary, goes back to 1316. Yet only a handful are pre-reformation. A few more are post-reformation but most are modern. A majority even of hereditary titles were created this century, 656, and an overwhelming majority if life peers are included. Mass political parties took over the political system from the 1860s and today's House of Lords is their creation even though it is more palely political than the cockpit Commons.

Monastic land-grabbing, the provision of heterosexual sexual favours to Charles II or homosexual ones to James I, were the origins of some titles, but party politics have been the reason for most. In 1688, at the start of the Augustan age of the "Venetian Oligarchy" when the peerage effectively ruled England, there were only 160 Lords temporal. The number remained low until Pitt shaped a new Tory Party at the end of the 18th century but the needs of power then began an escalation of numbers which became more rapid with the growth of mass parties after the 1867 Reform Act. Parties used peerage patronage to reward and build support and, by the turn of the century, to raise money. This process culminated in Lloyd George's scandalous sale of honours which was only an overuse of processes then becoming a norm. So 194 new titles were created between 1900 and 1920, and the scale of changes is indicated by the first Baron Vestey who paid £20,000 for his title as late as 1922. Even when new rules outlawed cash-and-carry peerages, party politics remained a major reason for creation of peerages, though as a reward for services rendered, rather than hire purchase for services to come.

As parties created titles they weakened the House of Lords they were trying to control, for institutional power is in inverse ratio to numbers. That law makes today's Cabinet of 24 less powerful than it was, the Commons with 659 members fairly impotent, and the Lords with 1239 peers eligible to sit, plus 26 Bishops and 27 Law Lords, a total of 1292, almost powerless. The Lords are less powerful than they were and, symbolically, today's is their biggest membership ever.

The growth in members is due to the rapid growth in life peers, currently 509, but still increasing rapidly as Labour brings in more support. This rising tide compares to only nine hereditary peers of first creation: only four of them (one the Duke of York) created since 1964. The life peers do not outnumber the hereditaries yet. But they have already taken over power in the Lords mainly in the debates and the votes.

We were really the Geoffrey Howes of the 16th Century. Wealthy lawyers who came to better themselves in London. The real originator of my family's fortunes attached himself as an impoverished Welsh squire's younger son to the baggage train of Henry VII who came and defeated Richard III at the Battle of Bosworth. We attached ourselves to the courts of the Tudor monarch thereafter and by the middle of the century William Cecil, who later became Lord Burleigh, became indispensable as Clerk to the Privy Council and eventually chief minister to Elizabeth I, until Burleigh died in 1598. Then his second son, the first Lord Salisbury, succeeded him as Chief Minister and arranged the transition from Tudor to Stuart without any trouble.

We then managed to sink ourselves into oblivion with a series of completely half-witted Salisburys who dissipated what was left of the family fortune until we started marrying a series of very strong-minded and intelligent women which revived the family fortunes but more importantly, revived their brains. It's a vindication of the horse breeder's view that you must always look at the mare. This reached it's apotheosis with Prime Minister Salisbury, as he became, marrying a judges daughter. His father thought this was very 'not the thing', and cut him off without a shilling for marrying beneath him.

The most sensible thing he ever did. She was a formidably intelligent woman who bred a series of formidably intelligent children who were perhaps a little self-indulgent which meant that they didn't really reach the top flight in politics. I don't think there was any bloodline connection with the 16th and 17th century Cecils. It just happened that their descendents married some extremely formidable and sensible women.

Lord Cranborne, Conservative

It was a very big surprise. I was in France and it was the last night of the conference and my husband opened the letter which said, 'private and strictly confidential', and got very drunk. He rang me up and said, "you're going to the Lords". Of course, I had a sleepless night, couldn't tell anybody, and wrecked the next day. Thrilled to pieces and terrified.

Lady Trumpington, Conservative

I come from a Liberal background. My grandfather had been political at a local level but my father had always been pretty active in the 18 or so years that he was a member of this House, on the Liberal benches. So I always knew the Lords pretty well, and had no doubts about coming here. I did spend some time in local government after I inherited, as a county councillor in Cumbria, just before I went on the front bench in government. I came straight in. It took three months to establish my claim - one has to prove that you're the eldest son and all that, and that there are no other elder sons in the way or whatever. Obviously, if you inherit from more remote relations, it can take a lot longer. I started coming here to see what it was like and one gets rather gripped by it.

Lord Henley, Conservative

I had a call from Harold Wilson with whom I'd been in touch for many years on economic matters. I was afraid that he might be asking me to become a junior minister in the Lords which would, of course, have meant my giving up my practise and everything like that. So I spent about a quarter of an hour pacing up and down Downing Street hoping to God that he wasn't going to offer me a job. Fortunately he didn't. He said that he'd like to send me to the House of Lords and he thought I'd do a good job over there, but it'd be a working job and what did I think about it. I said, "Yes that'll be all right by me and you can rely on me to do a job of work".

Lord Bruce, Labour

My title is a Scottish one. I inherited it in 1975 from my father. It was created in 1114 and is the oldest title in Britain. I'm also the Premier Earl of Scotland. If I had a son he would be Lord Geary, because Geary is part of the Mar territory. And my daughter is the Mistress of Mar. Our title derives from the seven original princedoms of Scotland. They always knew who the mother was, but they didn't necessarily know who the father was. I think that it was probably a matriarchal society in ancient Scotland.

Countess of Mar, Cross-bencher

I was sitting in a chair in Ireland last June and I got a phone call from Number 10 asking if I would like to come to the Lords and my answer was "will it interfere with the work I'm doing because I've just got this lovely job working for David Blunkett?". The answer was "not necessarily". The job at the DOE would always take precedence. "As long as that's sure", I said, "Yes, that would be really interesting". It was absolutely out of the blue. Then, which is even funnier, from about the 6th or 7th of June I didn't hear a single word until I picked up a   newspaper at the end of August. Not a call, not a letter. I just assumed that perhaps it seemed like a good idea at the time, and they'd changed their minds.

Lord Puttnam, Labour

I succeeded my half-brother who was 15 years older than me. There was always the possibility either that I might inherit or that I might not. I deliberately made up my mind when I was quite young, I wasn't going to live with my tongue hanging out, so would not think too much about it. I inherited suddenly and unexpectedly at the age of 50 and my half-brother died rather young. I came here immediately into the Education Bill of 1988, and found that I liked the place immensely. I got involved more and more as I went on. What really struck me is that it's the Standing Order of this House that all peers count equal. And they do actually mean it. At least you count equal when you get up, whether you do when you sit down is up to you. I reckon we make almost no difference, but we make more difference than MPs do.

Lord Russell, Liberal Democrat

When my father died, I suppose I expected to inherit. But I'd retired from politics. I had been very briefly, an extremely obscure backbencher from '79 to '87. I didn't like the House of Commons very much. I thought it didn't do its job very well. I thought it was a bit wet only to stay for one parliament. So I thought to myself, well, I'll stay for two. That was reinforced by my dislike for the House of Commons.

With a sense of some relief I retired into doing my own thing in '87. I was absolutely astonished to be summoned in '92 and offered a junior job in Defence. Which meant coming here early. Major said, "Well, you'd better take a Life Peerage". So I said, "No, I won't do that". But he said, "You can't be a minister unless you're a member of one House or the other". So I said, "I know that, but there is another way which is a written acceleration". The reason why I was attracted by that was, quite apart from revelling slightly in the arcana, that it meant I didn't have to change my name again. Which would have been a hell of a bore. So I start off as plain Robert Cecil, my grandfather dies and I become Cranborne, my father dies assuming all this still exists so I become Salisbury. If I've got to have another change of name through life Peerage it's one too many. This was an admirable way of not having to do it again.

Lord Cranborne, Conservative

I came here because I'd been the party Chairman for the Liberal Democrats and Party President. I worked in the chemical industry for about 30 odd years before that and was a bit surprised when David Steel said, "I want you to go to the Lords". I thought well, I'm not going to get into Parliament through the front door; I might as well go in through the back door, and I've thoroughly enjoyed it. When I came the Liberal Party was only the old Liberal Party. There were 40 I suppose - about half of them hereditary peers. We had a very thin time during the Thatcher period when she didn't give us a single working peer nomination for nine years. We had one or two people through the honours list. I think she just didn't like Liberals.

Lord Tordoff, Liberal Democrat

I did want to come, though I would rather have carried on in the Commons. But it had got to the stage, looking at it in a practical way, when one thought being in the Commons was an uncertain business and if one wanted to remain in the swim, then the Lords was the place.

Lord Harmar-Nicholls, Conservative

In '83, I lost my seat in Edmonton, and Michael Foot was kind enough to have me put forward. He put forward more than 20 people for a list of working peers, and Margaret Thatcher wouldn't have it. She said it was out-rageous. "If you have 20, I've got to have 30", and that's no way to go. Finally, after the battle, she gave him seven. Five of those were ex-whips. Michael Cox was instrumental. He and Michael Foot decided that we need-ed people up here, and I always like to think we were sent up here as work-ers. Jock Stoddard, David Stoddart, Neil Carmichael, Joe Dean, and myself, all had been whips.

Lord Graham, Labour

It was given to my great-uncle in 1919 at the end of the First World War in recognition of his services in the Middle East, when the Ottoman Empire came to an end and Britain assumed the role of protector of the Middle East. I think if he'd not moved from the Battle of the Somme and Paschendale, he would have probably never been heard of again. Being a cavalryman, of course, in the open spaces of the Middle East, the desert, particularly suited his temperament and his way of doing things.

Lord Allenby, Cross-bencher

My father was the first baron. He was a member of the House of Commons for 19 years. My father died within a month of my 21st birthday. I couldn't come in straightaway because my older brother was missing, believed killed during the war, and it took about a year to get a certificate of presumption of death from the Air Force. I took my seat straightaway then and I was work-ing, I had two jobs. One in the Stock Exchange and then afterwards, one in Lloyds. I only started coming here regularly in the early to mid fifties. You get a sort of enthusiasm for the place before you come here.

Lord Denham, Conservative

I don't think I'd thought about coming here. I hadn't particularly wanted or particularly not wanted. At the end of his government in 1976 Harold Wilson had a private chat with me to suss out if I wanted to come here. But my col-league Joe Haines had already said no, so I didn't take that up and after that, I didn't give it a lot of thought. When I was approached about it I was then working in the City, and I missed politics and I thought it would be attractive to continue being in the political stream. If one's been in politics a long time, it's actually hard to go completely out of it. I found being in the City I was a bit isolated. So it was quite attractive.

Lord Donoughue, Labour

The title was created at Queen Victoria's Coronation. The first Lord Sudeley was a good Whig, and Lord Melbourne's administration was somewhat shaky. He was the Chairman of the Commission for rebuilding the Houses of Parliament. I inherited at the age of two. I was introduced when I became of age but I didn't start taking it seriously until 1968 with the rather daunting prospects of reform. They were ditched in 1969. So one felt a bit safer being here.

Lord Sudeley, Conservative

I was delighted to come here because I was stuck on the GLC after Ken Livingstone became leader and I was left with nothing to do, politically. Livingstone had the theory that you give the chairmanships to your political mates and he left me as a member of the Police Committee and nothing else. So my first thought when I was called in here was, thank goodness I can resign from the GLC. Michael Foot, who I kept in contact with after the GLC election, was very angry at what Livingstone had done. Consolation prize sounds as though it was some sort of handout. What he thought, I think, was I had things that I could do for the party that I could no longer do in the GLC, but the House of Lords might be a place to do it.

Lord McIntosh, Labour

I'd expected to come here since the age of 12. My father was created one of the last hereditary peers and up until then I had a cousin who'd got the peerage. I wasn't his heir. I've always known them quite well with being closely related to them, but I've never been in the position where I thought I actually might get it. So it was only when I was 12 or 13 that the possibility of coming here really crossed my mind. I was in a very awkward position because I stood for the European Parliament and I was elected. The count was held on a Sunday night and my father died on the following Thursday. He was very ill during the campaign, and I told him I'd won - just - on a recount, and he was semi-conscious, but he understood. So I had a pretty strange week. Because I was elected to go to Europe that was my priority. I made my maiden speech here, and that was really all I did until I lost the following European Parliamentary election. I was put onto the frontbench and the whips' office shortly after.

Lord Inglewood, Conservative

We come in by seniority, most of us. Five bishops go in automatically on appointment, that's the two Archbishops and then London, Durham and Winchester and the other 21 of us wait our turn by seniority of appointment and it's an automatic pick-up. You wait about five to six years on average. I waited just about 6. So I've just done over four now. I regarded it as a bit of a nuisance at the beginning, but I've grown increasingly to enjoy it. It's been a very interesting time to be in the Lords and I think the Lords have been able to make some contribution to legislation and to life. Being away from London, it's very nice to have a good London base. It is a very good club.

Bishop of Lincoln

We were cattle thieves in the Welsh-Shropshire border in the 10th century. We Became mildly respectable and then in 1560 the younger son, the then senior Onslow in Shropshire, had taken advantage of the early property boom and made a lot of money. He came down here, married an heiress at Merle and also became Solicitor General and Speaker. He was the first Speaker over whom the House of Commons ever divided because they said as Solicitor General he had been servant of the House of Lords rather than the House of Commons. Anyway, Queen Elizabeth got her way. Since then we've had three Speakers in the family.

Earl of Onslow, Conservative

It was hardly my life's ambition. I managed to avoid running for Parliament despite a life time in politics, one way or another. I did actually want to be part of the Labour government and when Tony and I discussed whether I should move on from being General Secretary he did indicate that I had the possibility of the Lords. I did not demur. I expected that to happen some time during the Labour Government. In fact, I was in there for six months before the Labour Government. I'm quite glad I've done it; I've gone in, I play a minor part in the Labour Government, but it's quite nice at this stage of life to think you're actually speaking for the Government. In that sense, I'm happy to be here.

Lord Whitty, Labour

The title was given to my father who was a Conservative MP who moved too far left for the comfort of his party. What happened was that when he was Minister of Health and Housing he refused to pay compensation to slum own-ers on compulsory purchase. You don't compensate the butcher when you confiscate fly-blown meat in the market place do you? That was remembered against him and so when the next general election came in 1935 he was pushed upstairs. I did expect to go to the House of Lords. I was 30 so I knew that it was coming, I knew I had to do something about it.

I didn't look forward to it. My father was 45 years older than me and at that time if you were in your were in, you couldn't disclaim. So I made the decision early on that I wasn't going to waste my time winning elections because when my father died at an expected age of 75 or 80 years I would go into the Lords. The only alarm came really with the Enabling Act but by then I was caught between two stools. I did think of renouncing it when I inherited. I thought very carefully and very nearly did renounce it. Finding myself in doubt I went and consulted Harold Wilson. Should I renounce? He said, "No, you go in. We're going to need you", and then I thought that if it's prevented me working on getting into the Commons all these years, why not accept what's on offer under the amazingly incredible and utterly medieval constitution. So I did accept.

Lord Kennet, Labour

I actually learned about it in August of last year at Downing Street at a garden party. I was talking to Ken Dodd, the comedian, and Stuart Pearce, the Nottingham Forest football manager, and John Major came up to me and said, "John, do you mind if I take you away from these two?" I was talking to two of my heroes. But when the Prime Minister asks you a question you don't say no. So we walked around the garden just the two of us, leaving the other 200 behind and he then said, "What would you feel about going to the House of Lords as a peer?" I was a bit gobsmacked. Then he explained why. He said "Look, we are looking for lawyers; I want to bring down the average age." He was at pains to say, "This is not because you are black. That is going to be put to you, but I am telling you now that it's not because you are black." I didn't argue with him.

Lord Taylor, Conservative

My ancestor, the First Earl of Glasgow got his peerage in 1703 and he was very much involved with the Union of the Parliaments which is extremely controversial at the moment and we're rather disliked by the Scottish Nationalists. In fact the Earl of Glasgow is rather vilified by Scottish Nationalists because he was meant to be the one that got a lot of money from the court of Queen Anne and bribed a lot of these Jacobites in the Scottish

Parliament to vote for the Union of the Parliaments. It's very unlikely, historically, that Scotland would have agreed to the Union of the Parliaments if there hadn't been an oiling of the wheels, and the Earl of Glasgow has always had the reputation as one of the people who was responsible for bribing them. But I've always thought in fact that there's nothing intrinsically wrong with bribing people in a good cause. I think that it's the people who actually take the bribes who should look to their consciences.

Earl of Glasgow, Liberal Democrat

I never expected to come here. I'd been in local government for 15 years and I was on the Party Candidates' list. I applied for a seat for which I wasn't selected. But at the time I had three children, one only eight years old and I realised that it was impossible to conduct a life in London, have a home in Oxford, and a constituency miles away. Some people could manage all that, but I realised I couldn't. The 1970 election came and went and I was on the point of trying once again to find a seat for the Commons, when, to my complete astonishment, I got a letter from Ted Heath saying that he had it in mind to nominate me as a life peer to the Queen. Nobody could have been more surprised than I was. I realised that this was a wonderful opportunity and certainly one that I'd never expected, and I accepted. Within a year of arrival in the House, I found myself on the front bench and I did two years under Edward Heath as Prime Minister and eight under Margaret Thatcher.

Lady Young, Conservative

We originally came from Suffolk and had great good fortune there. A Cavendish married Bess of Hardwick. She had four husbands, all of whom had property, and by great good fortune she only had children by Cavendish. So we got the lot. We always played it safe and in due course, in the 17th Century, we were made Earls and then, in 1688, we backed William and Mary against James II (we were very staunch Protestants). Again we played it safe, we didn't go over to Ireland to fight in the Battle of the Boyne, we stayed at home but we were still made dukes for it.

Our family motto is "Cavendo Tutus"? which is not only a pun on the family name but it means 'safety by caution' and, my word, haven't we stuck to it.

Duke of Devonshire, Cross-bencher

This particular peerage, Strange, was created in 1628 by mistake. The eldest son of Lord Derby was called to the House of Lords as Lord Strange. It was

28

created by writ for him and he was in fact a friend and supporter of Charles I,. His wife was a lady-in-waiting to Henrietta Maria, and they both fought for Charles I in the Civil War. He got beheaded for it at Bolton in 1651, so it didn't do him any good. I'm the third woman to sit in the Lords because it went from the Derby family - it finally died out because it goes to the nearest heir and if there isn't an heir, a male heir, then it goes to the female. Supposing there was a Lord Strange and he only had daughters, like my father, then it would go to one of the daughters. I am the oldest daughter, but it isn't automatic because under English peerages there is no right of primogeniture for females since the reign of Henry VI. So we are all equal, we all have an equal share and claim, and we have to agree amongst each other without impropriety, which means that I don't say, "here's 50 quid, let me be Lady Strange". As long as you don't do that, and as long as you agree, then you have to prove that your father had no son, and then you have to petition the Queen. It all takes quite a long time. It took us four years.

Lady Strange, Conservative

The second Viscount was King Charles I's principal Secretary of State, which meant that he was his personal advisor. James I, who created my peerage, created a number among his own personal friends because he was, to put it in inverted commas, "an affectionate man". I'm happy to say that my ancestor was not of that circle, but he valued him as an administrator. Which is probably why he got a Scottish peerage and not an English one.

Viscount Falkland, Liberal Democrat

My great-grandfather was involved with the Lloyd George Government, and they offered him a peerage. It was early Lloyd George, so it wasn't one that we paid for. The later Lloyd George ones were bought. I inherited rather unexpectedly because my father was only 52/53 when he died in 1967. I was 24, just qualified as a dentist, and had to change all my writing paper and everything, so it was a shock to me. I did go and take my seat in the House of Lords as my stepmother insisted, but actually didn't get terribly involved. It wasn't until about ten years later, in the middle 70s, that I realised that it was something I could get involved with and that's when I started becoming involved with the House of Lords.

Lord Colwyne, Conservative

It is by writ to heirs general, so obviously it's to males first, but if there aren't any males then it goes in the female line. You're a co-heiress, so if there is more than one female, it's between the two of you so one has to stand down, and it's usually the younger one that does stand down. I mean I have a sister, and she stood down and so I became the next one. But it has to go before the Solicitor General and you have to petition the Queen, and she has to agree. I inherited it from my mother and she inherited it from her brother. He died in 1969, and he didn't have any children, so then it went to my mother and she didn't sit here because she lived in Portugal.

Lady Wharton, Cross-bencher

My peerage is quite a recent one. I'm the fourth peer. My great-grandfather became a peer in 1930. He'd been a Labour MP and a minister. My grandfather was a Liberal. He came here, but he never spoke. My father was Labour as well, and was very active. He was the Chief Whip here for the Labour Party while they were in opposition. I very nearly didn't come here. I was a Labour councillor at the time, my father died quite young and unexpectedly. So I hadn't really been thinking about it at all.

The way the procedure works is you've got a year to give it up. If you don't do anything within a year then it's yours for the rest of your life, but if you actually renounce it within a year then you put it into abeyance until, in my case, my son would take it up. I was very ambivalent about whether to take it. The way I characterised the choice to me was a choice between principle and opportunity. I asked a lot of people about what I should do, including Neil Kinnock, and in the end I chose opportunity. It's not something I regret. I do think I have done some useful work while I've been here, and I hope to do as much again.

Lord Ponsonby, Labour

It was conferred for political services to the Gladstone Government. The first Lord Monkswell was a legal eagle in Gladstone's Government and set up the judicial committee of the Privy Council and was one of its founder members. The second Lord Monkswell was a founder member of the LCC, and a radical Liberal at the turn of the century. The third Lord Monkswell was not really political, but was very keen on steam railways and promoted them. The fourth Lord Monkswell was my father, he inherited in '64 and, having been a Labour councillor for 17 years, a socialist, felt the House of Lords should not exist, and disclaimed the title. I automatically inherited the title, so I was the fifth Lord Monkswell. I knew at the age of 16 when my dad inherited that I would eventually inherit and that I would take my seat. I am, by nature, a joiner, getting involved in things, changing things from within, rather than standing outside and throwing stones. All I inherited was the title and a set of robes.

Lord Monkswell, Labour

It's not very often that, in your later 40s, you find yourself being treated like a young girl. But given that the average age here is in the eighties, it was slightly like appearing in a sort of 1930's musical comedy. As an individual I was delighted to come because I stood as a parliamentary candidate in Great Yarmouth and I'd been offered a safe seat for the '83 election. But because my children were ten and twelve and I thought I would end up with a constituency possibly in the Midlands and a home in Norwich, and trying to work in Westminster, I wouldn't have a marriage or much of a life. So when Roy Hattersley, a couple of years later, said would I go to the Lords, I said "thank you very much". Then Maggie Thatcher refused to appoint anyone for three years so I didn't come in 'til 1990. Then I found within three months I was being a whip and within six months I was doing a front-bench job.

Lady Hollis, Labour

I think there is an advantage so far as wives are concerned, in terms of the attention they get in shops and so on, that the husbands probably don't know about. I don't think my wife married me because I had prospects of inheriting a peerage and she certainly didn't marry me for my money. The very week when my father died and I inherited my peerage she decided that she wanted to separate. We separated for a number of years and then divorced. My present wife is very, very diffident about the whole thing, because she works in the film industry, with tough rough people and she uses her maiden name. Once somebody did ring up for the Viscountess Falkland. Apparently though they were talking about a pub. It caused a great deal of confusion. So she's stuck with her maiden name.

Viscount Falkland, Liberal Democrat

In 1971 just after my father died, Bill Blydon who'd been MP for Seaham Harbour, was given a peerage. He told me he went home and said, "Joan, I'm to be Lord Blydon, you're going to be Lady Blydon". She went upstairs to bed, and he sat in the lounge watching telly. Fifteen minutes later, she came downstairs in a long, Victorian flannelette nightie. She said, "Watcha gonna be Bill?" He said, "I'm going to be Lord Blydon of South Shields". She said, "You've been that for the last 30 fuckin' years" and went straight back upstairs to bed again.

Earl of Onslow, Conservative

I've always had an overdraft, I've got a very small, very ordinary house and a great number of my colleagues and people just don't believe it. I was in Canada recently and they kept on asking me about my castle, and when I showed a photograph of my house, people didn't believe it. We are very ordinary run-of-the-mill people. There are people with large estates who also come to the House and contribute, and you can't differentiate between one and the other. But on the whole the majority of the hereditary peers are very ordinary people - policemen, servicemen, dentists, orchestra leaders. There are people from very rich backgrounds - some have fallen on very evil times. History is extraordinary how it repeats itself. Yes, there are rich people who contribute, but you wouldn't know they were rich. They are very ordinary people.

Lord Allenby, Cross-bencher

Coming to the Lords was something that I knew would happen eventually. But it came as a complete surprise and I sort of fell in to politics rather than being very political before coming here. Everybody expected that I was going to become a Conservative, because my father was a Conservative whip. And the day I took my oath I decided I wouldn't join the Conservatives and I went down and joined the Liberal Democrats. In fact some of the Conservative peers didn't speak to me for a couple of years. To start off it is a very strange place although it's changed now and it's becoming more political. In the past it was a very much less political place. You would go along, become a member of a political party or become a cross-bencher and do your work in the Chamber, but outside it had the feeling of a club.

Lord Redesdale, Liberal Democrat

When I first came here people who were not hereditary peers said to me, "We're not proper peers, we're only life peers", and I said to them, as I say it now to the life peers, "the difference between us is that you achieved your title by merit but we achieved ours by no merit. Therefore we have to work that much h,arder to show that we are some good". The great thing about this

House is that everybody is equal, and if you're a duke or a life peer or a hereditary peer, or whatever you are, you're all equal.

Lady Strange, Conservative

It's a bit like a sort of warm bath to start with because it's quite comfortable. Peers are very clubbable, everybody tries to make you feel welcome. I hope in particular that they try to make Labour peers feel welcome. Not just out of politeness but, of course, we are all very keen that they should be native. Which a large number of them do. So there is method in that politeness as well.

Lord Cranborne, Conservative

I enjoy it and it's a very agreeable second best to being in the House of Commons. It is a sort of political life after death. When Neil offered to put me up for a peerage I said, "Thank you very much indeed, you're offering me a new lease of life". He said, "It's not a lease it's a freehold life". So, in a sense, one is very fortunate that one can still be active in politics after normal careers have, perhaps, come to an end. I do like it up here and I think the Lords, on the whole, does a worthwhile job. I do not think the composition of the Lords is acceptable, but the actual functioning of the thing in looking at legislation in the way that it does, opening up subjects that are perhaps a bit too sensitive for the House of Commons, giving a platform for retired Field Marshalls or ex-Permanent Secretaries and that sort of thing I think is useful and is worth keeping.

Lord Richard, Labour

The Lords has changed. There's a higher proportion of life peers, and the aim is not quite so high as it was. Sometimes people come here because they've made a name for themselves as party activists in various parts of the country - no harm in that - and that's true on the Labour side as well as on the Conservative side. At first they may feel disillusioned when they get here but eventually they understand the form and they stop being so militant. They then fall into the customs of courtesy and being constructive.

Lord Renton, Conservative

If you actually look at where the initiative and momentum come from, where power lies in this organisation, it is, with one or two exceptions, with the life peers. It must be historically quite an interesting evolution to go back to 1958 when this change came in and to see the way that the power within the system has been shifting from hereditary peers to life peers. Which means if a change comes forward and only the life peers remain, the continuity of the system will be much more than some outsiders might think. It must have taken quite a long time to get a critical mass. But now if you look at the people who influence the House, take the decisions that affect the House on the issues that matter, it's the life peers.

Lord Inglewood, Conservative

You don't get anything like the tea room divisions that you get in the Commons where we're shoved at one end and the rest go down to the other part. They all mix together quite freely and I normally have coffee in the morning with a Liberal, a Tory whip and an Independent. Sometimes even with my own side. Socially it's a very pleasant place to be in. The feuds are virtually nil.

Lord Bruce, Labour

You can tell who's hereditary and who's a lifer now because there are a lot of people coming in, and so there's a kind of cliquey atmosphere. When I came in in 1990 it was just like a wonderful melting pot and it all sort of swirled around and everybody melted into each other. Joe Dean of Beswick, who has been here for a very long time, once said to me, "Now Ziki", he said "the wonderful thing about this place, it's the most democratic place on earth, and we're all equal". I thought that was wonderful. And it actually is true, but now there's a different atmosphere.

Lady Wharton, Cross-bencher

CHAPTER THREE

Welcome to the Club

THE House of Lords is a legislative club for amateurs. Its entry rites, traditions and rituals are all designed to awe and impress as if the members were
in fact powerful professionals and the House a repository of historical wisdom
and real power in all its majesty. Yet a basic British constitutional device is
deceit. Politics, like Victorian piano legs, are best concealed, lest the sordid
reality shock a deferential nation. So they are conducted in a cathedral to
inspire awe and confer respectability.

That subterfuge is exploited by both Houses but the Lords do it better.
Certainly much more to the satisfaction of the electorate, and even more so of
its own members. They enjoy the job, feel they're doing it well, and want to
go on doing it: important or impotent. Most don't particularly mind being
overawed by entry rites designed to persuade them, and the world, that they're
joining a mystical brotherhood and a club worth belonging to.

———————————

I came in and met the Chief Whip and the Leader and Ted Graham. Then I
had to have a meeting with the Garter King of Arms, who had a face of
Dostoevskyian melancholy. I'd decided with the Battersea Labour Party that
I would call myself Lord Dubs of Wandsworth, because they already had
Douglas Jay as Lord Jay of Battersea. So I said to him tentatively that I'd
thought of Lord Dubs of Wandsworth. He spent 20 minutes trying to explain
to me that in every institution there's a pecking order, and what he didn't like

to say to me was that I was at the bottom of the pecking order in the Lords, so you can't be so grand as to attach to your name a whole local authority. If you are a duke you could be the Duke of Northumberland or the Duke of Westminster. But if you are at the bottom of the pecking order you can only have a part of a local authority. Wandsworth, therefore, was way above my station. I had to settle for Battersea which, although it used to be a borough, is now simply a part of the Borough of Wandsworth. The attachment of the geography is only to distinguish between people of the same surname. So it doesn't matter really because no one has a surname like mine.

Then I had to have various meetings with people who explained things to me, the Clerk of the Parliaments and so on. Then came this terrible ordeal which is the introduction. You have to wear this sort of red thing with ermine, and some of the animal rights people immediately lobbied me before my introduction and asked if I would take a stand against wearing ermine. I asked the Chief Whip if anybody had ever refused to wear the gear and he told me that if they did they wouldn't be able to take their seats.

You have to rehearse your introduction. Ted Graham was anxious to get us in quickly because he needed the votes for the divisions. First we had to watch a video of someone else doing it as it's a complicated bit of choreography. Then we rehearsed it in the lunch hour, and you have your friends in for lunch so as it's a bit of an occasion. Then they go off to watch it from the public gallery.

I felt such a blithering idiot because I was wearing this thing with a funny hat and the Labour peers apparently mark you out of ten as to how well you do. You have two people to introduce you. They all have to wear the gear too. Then you do the thing, trying to remember desperately what the video showed. You're on your own after half an hour's training. At one point you are on the backbenches and have to sit down, stand up, bow, and again the Garter King of Arms with that air of Dostoevskyian gloom kept saying, "Sit down. Bow. Take your hat off". I knew my daughter in the public gallery was giggling and I could not keep a straight face, it was excruciatingly embarrassing, complete nonsense.

Unless I'm wearing the same gown, the same gear, I can't ever get to the State Opening of Parliament. I either have to wear the robes or I can't watch it at all. If you want to borrow them, you can hire them for 80 or 90 quid a day. Or you can buy them for about 600 or 700 quid. I think it's all ridiculous.

Lord Dubs, Labour

36

It was very peculiar coming here. First of all, the whole place seemed to me mustier. Every time I came in the door there was the smell of it and my heart sank. Quite honestly I thought it was an extraordinary place to work. The people you have to work with were really here to entertain their friends to lunch and dinner. I found it very easy to get used to the work.

I made my maiden speech on something which had nothing to do with the GLC. I spoke about the Ordnance Survey which I happen to know something about because I'd done work as a market researcher for the Ordnance Survey and I had fixed ideas and was opposed to the privatisation of the it. So I was able to speak in that debate and indeed we had a vote and we won. Then I followed that up by going onto the front bench to do Trade and Industry, determined not to be the person who had been kicked out by Ken Livingstone.

Lord McIntosh, Labour

If you inherit something or you get something in some way, then you've got a duty to do something about it. Whatever it is in life you're given you've got to do something with it, I reckoned it was a duty and because of that I ought to do something for other people. It meant I had to come down here and start thinking about it. I was a bit worried about it to begin with because my father was first of all a very amusing speaker. I knew that I couldn't face up to that because I'm not very amusing. The second thing is that he and Lord Boothby and Lord George Brown used to drink a lot of port after lunch. I'm not really into drinking port. But then I realised that you didn't actually have to drink port, and you didn't actually have to sit there after lunch a long time. You didn't even actually have to have lunch. What you had to do was to go and listen to what other people were saying and make up your own mind. It was a very interesting thing to do. I can't speak for more than five minutes because my knees shake too much, and I have to sit down because I get terribly nervous, because everybody knows everything about everything. And if you get up and say something and you don't know about it then you're much better not to speak.

Lady Strange, Conservative

It felt very peculiar at first. A culture shock. The second thing you notice is that people are very nice here, genuinely nice and helpful and there's not much aggro here, or if there is, it's beautifully phrased. There are ways of saying very rude things without being rude. It's not so much that it's a club there is a bit of that about it too of course. It is a working place, but people are extremely friendly to each other. They obviously have their differences, and argue it out but it's all done in a rational sort of way. I think partly because we are a self-regulating House. The Lord Chancellor, or whoever's on the Woolsack or in the chair in committee, does not keep order. That's the responsibility of the House itself.

Lord Tordoff, Liberal Democrat

When I first came up I found the atmosphere quite different. For one thing the party game was not played so hard. It's a much more friendly place, a much more civilised place. People make shorter and better speeches and can be very generous to each other across the floor of the House. You don't get any rudeness because it's utterly frowned upon. I didn't rush into making my maiden speech, I waited a month or two. When I had made my maiden speech I settled down and I've played a fairly active part ever since.

Lord Renton, Conservative

I was delighted. I couldn't believe how red it was. The carpets are plush. Phil Harris, Lord Harris of Peckham, would have a field day here. I thought, "Wow, he's in business here". But the sheer decor is really beautiful. I felt a certain amount of guilt as well. I'm aware of the fact that it's a very privileged position. I'm the only African Caribbean out of 1,200 so I'm not exactly the majority. The white community are comfortable with success, because it just happens. In the black community you really do stand out. My overall feeling is one of elation. With a slight feeling of "look, I'm the only one" and feeling slightly guilty. But that doesn't trouble me a lot because I'm there and I've got to make the most of it. I think the House of Lords needs people like me who aren't white - not from that stereotypical background - to bring creative ideas to it. I'm the only black lord in the world. So that's a great attraction.

Lord Taylor, Conservative

The next thing is your maiden speech. I was told to keep it to six or seven minutes, otherwise it was like the Commons and don't be too controversial. I spoke on the Queen's Speech debate soon after I was put in. They actually congratulate you and say they want to hear more of you. It's all lies of course. Mostly lies anyway. I had a job not making the same maiden speech I'd made in the Commons. There is one respect in which speaking in the Lords is more difficult. In the Commons you can stand up and say this is a matter of concern to my constituents, and everyone will forgive you if you make a second or third rate speech because they'll say, "OK if it's for constituency consumption". But in this place you don't have that excuse. Beneath the veneer of politeness they judge you much more critically, so in some ways it is actually tougher speaking here because the speech has to stand on its own.

Lord Dubs, Labour

It was terrifying. I did what I think more people ought to do and that is make the maiden speech in a quiet little debate, probably late, when nobody's there, instead of making a great, big showpiece of it. I spoke on housing for the elderly and because I thought nobody ever spoke about it, I discussed incontinence as being one of the real difficulties of the elderly. If you ever go round an old people's home, you're very conscious of it. Everybody laughed, well, all nine people who were there. I thought, why are they laughing? It wasn't until afterwards that I was told that, as I started talking on that subject, the heavens opened and all they could hear was rushing water. So I ploughed on. But anyway, I did it. I was very glad to get it over, because you do get a bit neurotic thinking about it.

Lady Trumpington, Conservative

I was very brave, I made my maiden speech on Suez, which was a brave thing to do. I was wrong, all the Tories were wrong. I'm one of the cross-benchers now but all Tories, rightly, are ashamed of Munich. I think Munich was the defining moment of my political life. The Tories were wrong on Munich and it's a lasting shame. But they over-reacted to Nasser and equated him with Hitler. They said, "We gave way to that dictator we're not going to give way to another" Had there not been Munich the Tories wouldn't have reacted to Nasser as they did. That's why I spoke in favour of it.

Duke of Devonshire, Cross-bencher

I made my maiden speech winding up for the Government on the last day of the Queen's Speech debate here. Which I think was the most terrifying moment of my life. I'd never spoken from a dispatch box before. It was certainly even more frightening than the maiden speech in the House of Commons. With my father watching me balefully from behind. But he was very restrained afterwards.

Lord Cranborne, Conservative

I came in November, I got my maiden speech over the night before Christmas. I just wanted to get it out the way, and we came back late January. I was very uncomfortable. I just kept waiting for someone to tap my shoulder and say, "Alright, back to real life". And after a while I suddenly, very quietly, felt good about it . I'd listened to a very good debate, I'd listened to a fantastic speech, and I suddenly felt good. I didn't feel too intimidated, I didn't feel odd, I felt this was fantastic, I actually have an opportunity to contribute and felt part of the process. It took six months.

I come from a theatrical world therefore the theatricality of it is not alien to me. People love film sets, partly because they're false but I understand that. It is theatre but I've been knocked out by some of the quality of the stuff. I love the politeness of the place. You get the feeling here, that, if in doubt, people are nice. It's the first time I've been in an environment that does not feel competitive. And it's wonderfully relaxing, hard to explain actually. My missus says "Do you realise that for the first time in your life you've got a base?" It's true. I've been a gypsy all my life in the film world with all the places that I go to. Now I have a sense of belonging.

I've spent the last six months negotiating quite a complicated arrangement which clearly is sensible but has a fair amount of opposition attached to it from some sections of the public. I've been able to invite whole groups of people here to have tea. There's such an air of reasonableness about the place and a kind of decency that people leave feeling it. It makes the event pleasant and I now have the ability to navigate difficult situations I could never have done in any other way. It may sound silly but what struck me at the moment I came in at the opening of the doors, was the image of my grandmother on her knees scrubbing doorsteps. I just found it a very moving thought. It would have been absolutely beyond her ability to imagine it. The nation has changed to a point where the unimaginable is possible. In her lifetime it would have been impossible.

Lord Puttnam, Labour

Everybody was terribly kind. It is like being in a huge family. Or it was, until recently. It's changed Because of this enormous influx of people who don't particularly want to be here. They don't have any feeling for the House, and don't really try to have a feeling about it. And it's sad. My friendships go entirely across party. People have been awfully good to me, really good, despite my misdemeanours. I never quite knew what was going to happen when I was answering questions as a minister. To go further back, when I first was made a whip, I was only, I think the second woman to become a whip, certainly in the Tory Party. When I used to come in, the men used to walk out. That's changed for the better. They weren't used to women. It was a men's club. Simple as that really.

Lady Trumpington, Conservative

When I first came into the chamber, sitting on the Labour benches looking across at the massed ranks of the Tories I suddenly found myself thinking, "He's dead, I'm sure he's dead" - and you realise that people you had thought died 20 years ago are still alive and sitting in the House of Lords.

Lord Monkswell, Labour

I was very impressed by its friendliness. I knew almost nobody when I arrived. I knew one woman life peer, Margaret Brook, and she was very kind to me. When I was getting myself introduced, I said I've got to have a second sponsor, and she said, "Henry will do it", her husband the former Home Secretary. So the two Brooks' were my sponsors and George Jellico, who was then Leader of the House, was very helpful and friendly.

I found people extremely friendly, interested to know what I'd done before I'd arrived, interested to know what I thought I might do having arrived. I felt a great sense of equality, particularly for women. I'd never been in an organisation where there has never been at any moment any sense of inequality between men and women.

In the dining room there's this long table and you simply sit where there's a gap. You talk to people who are sitting next to you. You introduce yourself and they introduce themselves, so the whole thing was very friendly. I was asked by George Jellico to get on and make my maiden speech and when I was going to do it I thought I was going to be ill. I was so anxious.

Lady Young, Conservative

I came here eight years ago. So I would have been 58. I felt just like a new boy coming back to school for the first time. I was very frightened, particularly when I was taken on one side by the Clerk of the Parliament and told I was talking too long on the floor of the House and would I shorten my speeches. I thought, my goodness, it's just like being had up before the headmaster.

Lord Allenby, Cross-bencher

I think the really toe-curling moments are when the House of Lords indulges in puerile and self-indulgent so-called humour on things such as red squirrels, pelicans in the park, chewing gum. You know in your heart of hearts that it's the only thing which the media are going to pick up on. The House of Commons has its puerile moments too but the House of Lords just doesn't realise what complete prats they're making of themselves. Also, of course, among both life and hereditary peers, there are some pretty silly people and you do hear some pretty silly speeches but that's inevitable in a parliamentary government. It's the House of Lords playing up to its nursery, old buffer, image which makes me most embarrassed.

Lord Cranborne, Conservative

I do have a more comfortable office than I had in the Commons. The Lords do have quite a number of offices. I share mine with three others but it's a very comfortable office and I have the full facilities there. There is also an excellent library and a parallel service in terms of the Commons. Certainly, the Lords don't receive the back-up that a Member of Parliament would now have, but that is right and proper. If you started staffing or equipping the Lords it would start to challenge the Commons.

Lord McNally, Liberal Democrat

It certainly wasn't the sort of place that I expected ever to be. When people ask what is the main difference between the Commons and the Lords I have to advise that the difference really is that in the House of Lords they actually listen to what you say. That can be frightening. On the other hand it can be productive because you can sway votes in the House of Lords. That's the charm of the Lords. It isn't fully party-politically controlled. The cross-benchers are highly intelligent. Many of them are very thorough. They do listen. They are very experienced and they will vote on an issue on its merits. Those are big differences. Also you don't have the 'yah boo' of politics in the Lords. Politics are conducted courteously and you can make your speech without being interrupted rudely, or being shouted at. There is the occasional lapse, and often I am one of the guilty parties, because it's very difficult to shake off the habits of a life-time in the Commons. It is a different place, but it's a very nice place. It's a place that I enjoy being in.

Lord Stoddart, Labour

I've almost learned to stop recognising people's age. Once you do that you find yourself at a long table having a discussion with the Bishop of Durham, Lady Warnock and, say, Lord Wilberforce, probably the best judge of the 20th century, and Robert Winston, talking about IVF and the ethics of IVF. You have those sorts of debates. I've had debates of a quality which are second only to British Academy in terms of the exponents. There are three or four people here who know opera, and people who paint superbly well, Law Lords, people who've run colonies, voluntary societies, local government leaders, former Secretaries of State.

I remember in my early days being involved in a debate on the Health Service in which I had three former Secretaries of State for Health. On any subject there are five or six people who've forgotten more than most civil servants will ever know. That is hugely impressive. Some of the contributions are pitiful but some of the stuff is infinitely better than in the Commons. We write our own speeches and people write from what they know, and they use pressure groups and lobbies, and their own information. The real difficulty with government is that all my information is on lend lease. I don't own it anymore. I found this hard to cope with. But there is real quality here.

Lady Hollis, Labour

A lot of the things that went on here were a surprise. Not the things that one had read about: the Lord Chancellor's procession, and the Ceremony of Introduction, the State Opening of Parliament. One is briefed about that and you've seen the State Opening on television anyway. I was aware of the building. I'm very interested in architecture and in Pugin because where I was born in Ireland, Pugin did a lot of work and I've always taken a lot of interest. I've always been a great supporter of Victorian Gothic. I think the craftsmanship was wonderful. But there were things that went on that I was completely thrown by and I think for the first six months I made a mistake every time I went into the chamber. Either getting up at the wrong time, not bowing at the right place, turning the wrong way, walking in the wrong direction, I was always being told off too by a fellow woman life peer. The men were much more tolerant. I think the women do it with the best possible motives but don't want to let the side down. What's wrong with tradition? I'm not an old fogey who wants to go into the waxworks but when you go abroad, a lot as I do, the first thing when you say you're a member of the House of Lords, they want to know about it. They are so envious of our whole parliamentary tradition. As a place to work it can be draughty and a bit anachronistic, but there are millions who'd give their eyeteeth to have the privileged position working here in Westminster.

Lady O'Cathain, Conservative

I wouldn't rather be in the Commons because I think in the Lords the standard of debates are higher. You've got experts in their fields speaking. When Lord Winston stands up and speaks in a health debate, especially about fertility, you don't yah-boo him - you listen. With great respect to the House of Commons, when most of them stand up it's to make political points. Ya-boo, on all sides. I just think it gets in the way of real progress.

In the Lords, everyone's made it. There's no sort of greasy pole to get up. So there are less egos flying around: I'm not saying there aren't any, but there is less backstabbing. There is respect for other opposing views and I think it's a much more healthy place and more conducive to getting things done. Its problem, in my view, is its P.R., in letting the public know about the hard work that goes on in here. The Lords are on the internet; they've got a fantastic library, they are very much into multi-media and I.T. Yet it's got a reputation of being in the 18th century, never mind the 19th. I think that needs improving.

Lord Taylor, Conservative

They say the House of Lords is dozy and doesn't have any power or whatever. This is not true. When you're on the committee on the floor of the House, you can actually change badly-drafted legislation. You can put arguments which make ministers of whatever government look at things again and bring it back to the civil servants and say perhaps we ought to look at this another way. I have seen quite a lot of things changed here by virtue of the expertise that is in this House. People can't really argue when you've got such tremendously expert people who say, "That's fine as legislation looks, as the drafting looks, but have you thought about a circumstance in which A should happen, and if A happens, well B almost certainly follows?" That is when you're at the committee stage of the bill and, indeed, from every other stage onwards.

Second reading almost seems to be party politics, but the line-by-line on the floor of the House is really great. I find that intellectually stimulating, I find it very rewarding. The hours are very long when you're involved with a bill, but solely because I think that I am making a contribution.

Lady O'Cathain, Conservative

The procedures are different and the atmosphere and style and culture are different. You actually have more chances to contribute and play a part than in the Commons, with less competition in the sense that one can always have a go at things. There are two things that are really better than in the Commons. One is that in a debate you put your name down to speak, none of this catching the Speaker's eye, because there isn't a Speaker. There's nobody to keep you in order which, again, I find difficult because I like to strain against the boundaries a bit. So you put your name down and they then divide the total time for the debate by the number of people and say that's your nine minutes or whatever time it works out at. That has some advantages because you know you are going to speak, and you know you are going to get called so you don't have this frustrating business that you have in the Commons of dancing up and down all day and then not getting called.

The second respect in which the Lords procedure is better than in the Commons is that there's a clock which tells you how long you've been speaking. If you do speak too long the whips point to their watches or nudge you and tell you time's up. Nobody can actually shut you up but there is pressure and the system is based upon a certain amount of co-operation. Because you are guaranteed a slot you have less wish to trespass on other people's time. Some people do go over the top a bit but there isn't a time limit for debate.

Lord Dubs, Labour

We actually do listen to each other. It's one of our great virtues as a House. Understood, occasionally. Discussed inside government, very occasionally. Acted on once in a blue moon. But I say that as somebody who has actually seen a blue moon.

Lord Russell, Liberal Democrat

In the Lords the votes are not scheduled at any particular time. We tend, by and large, to listen to the argument. I looked up my voting record the other day and saw of sixty votes I had only voted on fifteen occasions. That's probably because a lot of the time I was there and maybe abstained and thought, "No, I don't really agree with that". You use your mind and you work out what's best for the legislation.

Lord Colwyn, Conservative

I'm very fortunate. I've still got several non-executive directorships which keep me in touch with the business world and I find that ideal because I can bring some of the experience from there. Current experience, because a lot of people, particularly politicians when they come here, lose their political experience very quickly. People who are ex-civil servants, similarly, get out of touch very quickly, because life is changing so very much. But if you're still stuck in the middle of it as I am, with seven directorships, there's a sort of cross-transfer the whole time. Whitehall and Westminster have implications for all business. So if you are actually in the centre of it, in Westminster, it's very valuable.

Lady O'Cathain, Conservative

As for myself, who hasn't been able to do what I had wanted to do which is come through the Commons - because naturally I always wanted to be an MP - it's allowed me political responsibility and the opportunity to do what I think is a reasonably worthwhile job in. The degree to which you perform it actually makes a difference to the outcome in a way that's not true down the Commons. Yes, I find the clubby atmosphere beguiling, but beguiling in the sense that you can use it. People are here and they like to chat so you soften them up on things. You get them to agree that they're going to come in and listen.

Lady Hollis, Labour

Obviously, they do know a great deal about the law - I should bloody well hope so with the number of judges they've got. When the judges actually come and talk - Donaldson for example makes some bloody marvellous speeches, and Lesley Scarman when he had the ability - pure minted gold. So they do know a lot about the law and they talk a lot of sense about it.

If you leave out the law they are people who have worked very hard in their particular area. There are several doctors, medical men, who I've got a great deal of time for, who talk a lot of sense about euthanasia and all sorts of things that they've thought carefully about. The trade unionists? Well I must be careful. We've had good ones. Trade Union leaders are better in some ways if they've never been general secretaries because once they are general secretaries they're spoon fed. They've never made a speech off the top of their head in their lives since becoming general secretaries. It comes. There it is, and they've delivered it. They're not very good at making the set speech, the carefully considered, written down speech which is entirely their own work, so they're put off. They make their maiden, and one or two other speeches, and they bugger off.

Lord McCarthy, Labour

It's always bad being in opposition and it's always bad being part of the chamber which doesn't really decide things. But decisions are taken at different levels. Bevan always stated he went his way up from the urban district council looking for power and it was always one stage further away. We are one stage behind it and we always will be. On the other hand, it was a good thing for me in the sense that it enabled me to keep my amateur status. I always earned my living as a market researcher. I spent all this time both on a local council and on the Greater London Council as an amateur, earning my living somewhere else and not depending on politics for my living or even the centre of my daytime activity. Being in the Lords, I was able to continue doing that. Here am I at the age of 64 getting a paid job in politics for the first time in my life. Rather nice. The money's not great, but it's better than nothing especially on top of a pension.

Lord McIntosh, Labour

Harold MacMillan created life peers and that transformed the place. Until they came along business was over at five. It was a dead place, completely dead, but with the creation of life peers, my word it came to life. I sometimes wonder if the House of Commons didn't rather regret it because those who've been appointed will have their say. It became a very lively place with a very high standard of debate.

Duke of Devonshire, Cross-bencher

My Grandfather told me that before the introduction of life peers the place was dying on its feet and it was given an enormous shot in the arm by the introduction of life peers and particularly the introduction of women. The women here are terrific. From both sides. Margaret's very good, of course. Pat Hollis is terrific. Very good. And there are others as well. But what's happened is that very large numbers of former MPs have come in and I think that has changed the atmosphere a lot and for the worse. It's different. It's more party political and, in a way, the House shows itself best when it tries to rise above party politics.

Lord Cranborne, Conservative

It's a much better club than the House of Commons but the great advantage of the House of Lords is that it gives you a platform. It wasn't really different to what I'd expected because I'd been here lots of times to listen to them before I came in. It's not really a competitive place and it has influence because, on about a third of the amendments, the government accepts the Lord's decision. I think the debates are much better. They aren't so partisan or so predictable. After all, the whole purpose of the Commons is to have one side attack the other all the time. It's a much more relaxed place. I come in two or three days a week but I only speak on international finance, foreign policy and international affairs. I don't think anyone listens very much to what's said because they're not very well reported.

Lord Healey, Labour

There's no reason why peers should be dedicated. They're not paid. The main benefit of being a Member of the House of Lords is that you've got a parking space in the centre of London. They are qualified in ways that they could earn hundreds of pounds an hour. Yet they come here as part of what they see as their public duty, to do at a very low cost, the important job of scrutinising, revising and advising on legislation. I don't know what the Lords' expenses were last year but they would be no more than five million pounds. To get a second chamber, unelected or not, that's doing the job for five million pounds a year is very good value indeed.

Lord Stoddart, Labour

My measure of a professional, one hundred per cent, member of the House of Lords is one who writes and moves amendments. If you don't write and move amendments you are only here half-time because that's the work. You've got to be prepared to learn the system. A wonderful example of a great man who did it was Reg Underhill. Reg learned it from the ground up. Before he died he was Deputy Leader of the House, he had Transport and various jobs, and he was an absolute ideal example of a man who at his age - he was in his late 60s to 70s - just learned the whole damn thing from square one. Because he was modest, because he was intelligent, because he believed that if you had a job to do you did it, I call Reg a professional member of the House. Others won't do that. For them it's too demeaning. These people that we are selecting now, they won't do that. There's this rumour that half of them aren't members of the Labour Party, they won't come here and work, I'll bet you. Occasionally they'll vote and then they'll leak away, and there are no sanctions, absolutely nothing you can do. They just won't turn up.

Lord McCarthy, Labour

Chapter Four

Peers on the Job

THE House of Lords is a legislative sweatshop in which the most elevated in the land are exploited. Peers are persuaded to work practically for free by imposing on their sense of duty, their loyalty to their party, their anxiety to play a bit part in the big game of government, their desire to stay on the clattering train, and remain plugged in to politics, or even to life. Every emotion and attitude is exploited to the maximum to give Britain its cut price Second Chamber on the cheap. It's probably the cheapest in the world as well as the one with the oldest and most exploited workforce. The deal may be exploitative but it works.

Older peers confess that membership prolongs active life. All who attend feel they've got a useful job to do. So both sides of this cheap, posh club get something out of it: the peers get satisfaction (part time), while the executive gets the world's only cut-price legislature. They sit in a palace more opulent than any, to disguise the shoe string salaries, and so historic that it appears to go back even beyond Margaret Thatcher's days. Most people now view these as olden times so short has the institutional memory become.

The Lords work harder as amateurs than many more professional legislators. They sit four days a week, for 142 days a year. Neither this duty nor the work falls on all members, but on a hard core of regular attendees which now averages 376 a day - well up from the 136 a day in 1959-60 or the 250 a day during 1971-2, both before the chamber was televised. While 855 members attended at least once, only 286 (151 life peers and 135 hereditaries) attended two thirds of the sittings. This is the hard working core of peers who provide Britain with its second Chamber, on the cheap.

Members of the Lords work for little financial reward: pay peanuts get peers. No wage, just a daily allowance of £34.50 daily subsistence; £78.00 overnight allowance (paid only to those living outside London); and £33.50 secretarial allowance, making a total of £146 maximum for a day's attendance for a non-metropolitan peer. All this is tax-free which makes it a better perk for the well-paid than the pensioners, but spread over a year it is below the minimum wage and hardly a living, bringing in a maximum of £10,000 a year, earned by sitting every available day. Peers hardly do it for the money, which may be why the job is mainly attractive for to the independently wealthy. For instance those who can combine it with another job, or to pensioners as a gilded additional pension which now puts some in difficulties, like the third Baron Calverley. He was a Bradford policeman who retired from the force assuming that the Lords' allowance, on top of the police pension, would provide a decent living. Now he stands to lose half of it. Indeed, peers would earn more as full-time guides round the Palace rather than exhibits within it. This is why many peers take paid retainers from lobby groups, consultancies, causes or anything that offers.

As a result, the total cost of Britain's Second Chamber was only £38.5 million in 1996-7, comparing well on any Thatcher economy scale to £202.3 million for the Commons and £575 million for a European Parliament which is of even less visible use than the peers. Europe's travelling circus of a Parliament costs £918,000 per member, the Lords £37,000. The pay is also lower per hour. The Belgian, French and Italian second chambers cost slightly less than ours, but sit for much shorter periods and do less work.Like aged retainers living in the servants quarters of a stately pile, the Lords hesitate to ask for more for fear of being made redundant. Indeed, some use their cheapness, their role as the Kwik Save legislature as a line of defence.

The work for which they're paid so little isn't heavy. The House only occasionally sits beyond 10.00 pm and it rarely goes all night. Most of the work is light, sedentary, even trivial, important as the workforce themselves may feel it to be, while committee demands are comparitively light. Yet because all is so cheaply done, any reform must make the Second Chamber far more expensive, unless government is prepared to make an honest admission of the basic truth it has long kept well-concealed that pay is in direct ratio to power. By not having much, the Lords provide living proof of a principle which could be more widely exploited. Give senior citizens a role they think useful and they will do it for nothing very much, in much the same way as senior citizens toil at allotments and elderly Chinese citizens stand by the roadside to wave on passing traffic.

Being Leader in the Lords is a difficult job because we've got a 150 Labour peers and they've got nearly 500 Tory peers. So the only way in which you can function as Leader up here if you are in government, and in opposition as well to a certain extent, is to get on well with the other side. It's a totally different process from the House of Commons where they haven't got to like you but have to respect you enough to listen. Up here I think we go a good bit further because they'll listen to anybody. It is suffocatingly polite in that sense, compared to the House of Commons. You are heard here in silence, which I found very off-putting when I first came here, because if they actually listen to you, you have got to have something to say. So in that sense, it's a different type of chamber. As Leader you've got to be able to get along on decent terms with the other side because the essence of the job is management and consensus. If you are in opposition you've got to put coalitions together in order to defeat the huge Tory majority. If you're in government you've somehow or other got to stop them from voting. That requires a totally different set of skills to being in the Commons.

Lord Richard, Labour

This is a House that's built on consent. I get as annoyed as the next person when some elderly person roams on about a bee in their bonnet but though you can paint up the absurdities, it's actually run by people who are pretty professional. You take our front bench of ministers. Most of us would make office in the Commons. Many of them have had office: Stanley Clinton Davies, David Simon, all of these. People who are picked to do that job.

I find the House intelligent, generous, kind and tolerant. It's like family, the batty aunts, the ex-colonial types, whose prejudices aren't exactly veiled. The do-gooder, busy-body ones. It is slightly like the old Victorian family in the sense in which everybody has their roles cast and role plays, but most of the time I think it's a place you can do a rewarding job of work and that's quite a lot to me.

Lady Hollis, Labour

Although it does a good job of legislative work, it doesn't make much difference politically. I consider the place very marginal. Quite rightly government is run from the Commons in Whitehall and Downing Street and, frankly, most people there have no idea what's going on in the Lords. The only time anyone of the Government is aware of the Lords is when we get beaten. Then they come along and say, "Why did you get beaten?" But apart from that, I don't think we're of much consequence.

Occasionally we do things that matter. With Dennis Howell I helped organise the great defeat of the Conservatives and of Mr Murdoch over Satellite Television getting all the sports. We brought in the amendment that preserved a list of protected sports for the whole of public television. I did a great deal of networking with my Conservative racing friends, and suchlike, producing what someone told me was the biggest defeat for a Conservative government since 1906. Now I enjoyed that because that made a difference. It meant that the ordinary public could watch football and cricket matches, and the Derby on their television.

Lord Donoughue, Labour

Because we had this preponderance of Tories it would be embarrassing if too many people came too often. Everybody in this House has a job or an occupation outside. You are principally the thing that gives you a living and then, in a secondary way, you are a member of the Houses of Parliament. This is the thing that is going to be very difficult to preserve after reform.

Lord Denham, Conservative

The Gun Bill was a bloody awful bill and was really penalising law-abiding people. We had a colossal post on it. We don't get free postage. In the end I had to give up replying to the letters because it was getting too costly. Fortunately, Fiona Rippon, who looks after us, knows the sort of letters that we've had so well she sniffs out lobbies as opposed to the individual. I replied to, and still reply, to people who have written hand-written letters, but not faxes because it's very costly.

Lord Weatherill, Cross-bencher

The House of Lords usually sits for about 4 days a week. We sometimes sit on Fridays, particularly towards the end of the session, but I come up 4 days a week or certainly 4 afternoons a week. I work at home in the mornings, writing or looking at the previous days Hansards or preparing for committees that

I might be interested in, and I come up here and take part in all sorts of things, in questions if I'm interested in a bill. I spent a hell of a lot of time over the Child Support Bill trying to prevent what is now happening from happening. But it's not only that. If you're on a Select Committee then that's one afternoon out and Sub-Committee E meets on Wednesday. If we're doing an examination that's Wednesday out every week.

Lord Stoddart, Labour

I think we're seeing these new peers being created as working peers. Now to me a working peer is someone who is actually going to be there all the time - going to be there at two o'clock in the afternoon and work right through until late at night, because at the moment we are sitting through until midnight, or later, quite long hours. I want to see these new peers, working peers do that. I regard myself as an active peer. I go down there, but I only get involved in things that I know about. Now the working peers have got marvellous wide knowledge about everything, and there's a young guy who has come in - he's only 35, 36 - he runs a chain of discos or whatever it is. But is he going to be there as a working peer and give up everything else? I'm not sure.

Lord Colwyn, Conservative

I attend often partly out of a sense of duty and partly out of habit. Partly also, if there's something I believe I have to say on a case it's a way of getting it printed, then you can prepare 20 copies and send them out to people. Its mainly having a platform, reduced as it is compared with what it was because the press has stopped reporting, and the BBC have cut down their coverage. We are not shouting into a gale but into a press world completely dominated by non-political matters, which is ghastly. I still think it's a useful platform. Just. Sometimes the Government does listen if you make a case in a really convincing way, two or three times over. You've got to repeat it on at least two stages of the Bill for instance, but it is possible to make changes or to get assurances. The last one was the Land Mines Act where I managed to get the Solicitor General to come down to listen. One pleasure is the damn fine library. The club is dominated by the hereditaries. They outnumber the others in the bars and in the peers dining room, but not in the downstairs dining room which is cheaper.

Lord Kennet, Labour

I come here about three times a week. It's not regular. When we were in opposition I used to be here regularly three days a week and I used to spend two or three hours in the House on most occasions, using the excellent library facilities. But since May 1st, I've taken on another job which is to work as a special adviser to Margaret Beckett, so I now have an office over at DTI and I spend time working on DTI matters. Of course, the demands are greater in power and the organization is more demanding because, when you're in opposition, you call the shots. You decide when debates are going to take place. When you're in government you're at the mercy of the Opposition, instead of being able to know the vote is at 6.30 or 7.30 or even 11.30. Under our previous whip we used to have ambushes. Now, you know the vote is between four and seven. It may not take place at all. I share a division bell with Stanley Clinton-Davies. I hear it through my wall. It's like all busy people of which I'm one of many here. You can always find time to do something which can be valuable and useful.

Lord Hollick, Labour

I'm one of the little group which come about every second time there is a sitting; in other words, 60 or 70 days a year. So I'm neither an absentee nor a working peer - somewhere halfway in between. I usually come on Tuesdays and Thursdays. So long as I'm head of an Oxford College, which won't be much longer, I wouldn't be able to come on Wednesdays. At least not during term time, nor on Mondays.

I enjoy attending the chamber. I find many of the debates not only informative, but they change my mind about things. I like these debates. I do come like everybody else for questions and for the quick exchanges in the first half hour. But I take part in a debate no more than half a dozen times a year. I often come for lunch and sit on the long table there and talk to whoever my neighbours are and enjoy that too. I am on a Select Committee. I was on the European Select Committee which led me, although I should have known, to all sorts of new discoveries about a whole lot of things.

Lord Dahrendorf, Liberal Democrat

People do work very hard here. Everybody talks about these large sums of money people get for coming here. But you claim against expenses, that's the theory. And it's not all that much. If you can tell me where you can get a decent hotel in London for about £70 please let me know. Our secretarial allowance is only payable on the days that we attend. And we don't get any postage. We can use the telephones for free but only in the UK. We don't have constituency correspondence of course, and that's the reason that it's done that way. But we get quite a lot of correspondence from outside lobbying us on various issues.

Lord Tordoff, Liberal Democrat

I come four days a week. I'm totally committed, and when I came, I made up my mind that I would be useful and work and if I couldn't fulfil that, I wouldn't come. I didn't see the point. I certainly don't see it as a social thing because I don't use it that way. I find the older I get, I'm mentally becoming a bit sharper than I was 20 years ago.

I don't have to worry about family and children. It's a commitment. I don't think you can come here unless you're prepared to make a commitment. If there's nothing totally interesting I will spend quite a lot of time in the library, but it just so happens that nearly every day there has been something of interest, being on the animal welfare grouping as well. For a long time I was on Ian Ewing's Broadcasting group which started during the Broadcasting Act monitoring the BBC and ITV on taste, decency, sex, bad language and violence. Then I was heavily involved in the Dangerous Dogs Amendment, Douglas Houghton's amendment bill. That took a lot of hard work and about five and a half to six years to get the amendments to the mandatory death sentence. I regard that as quite an   achievement. And then I've got Pets Advisory Committee - a regular, once every six weeks. Then of course, there's the Media group and the issues that come out of that. Even with the four days a week there is actually an awful lot to do. And then there's entertaining, but it's usually on behalf of somebody.

Lady Wharton, Cross-bencher

You are paid so much per day for when you attend, and most certainly I do collect it. Anything that I am entitled to from any source, providing it's legal, I have it, down to the last farthing. I do that deliberately and with some enthusiasm because every penny they can take from me, they take.

Lord Harmar-Nicholls, Conservative

I don't collect my attendance allowance. I can afford not to. I don't see why I should be a burden on the taxpayer, that would be too much. I'm a lucky man. I'm well off and I don't need the money so it'd be a scandal if I was to take it.

Duke of Devonshire, Cross-bencher

Of course I collect my allowances. It doesn't matter if it's the House of Lords or an agricultural subsidy, I'm a great believer that if we're stupid enough to put troughs in people's faces, there's no possible reason why they shouldn't put their snouts in the troughs and both front feet, trotters and their floppy ears as well. I've said that on the floor of the House. If we're given an allowance it probably doesn't cover the extra expense to which one goes to come here.

Earl of Onslow, Conservative

Anybody who actually works on a regular basis here usually doesn't have a great deal of money. If you have vast wealth, people don't tend to turn up. It's one of the interesting things that in the past there was always this assumption that you had to be rich to be a peer. But most people now, due to death duties, aren't very rich. I have some land up in Northumberland which I run as a small estate and I run a couple of companies. I've met some peers here who have got their pensioner's bus passes and who actually try to live on the allowance. So some are very poor indeed.

Lord Redesdale, Liberal Democrat

It helped. It sure as hell helped. It isn't all that small. If you come regularly, it's not taxed. I attend regularly. Well, let's be honest, I need the money.

Lady Trumpington, Conservative

I'm paid less as a minister than any, even the 25 year old MP just come into the House. But we weren't paid in opposition at all. It was quite frustrating. I remember in '92, after the election, I realised I faced another five years just as an opposition spokesman in the House of Lords, which I enjoyed but never thought was of any great consequence. That was frustrating. But I also had to learn my subjects. I didn't have to learn Treasury, but Energy and the National Heritage. I worked on them. There are always things you could find to do here in the House of Lords, if you've got the time available.

Lord Donoughue, Labour

It's low pay for backbenchers. It's not reasonable to expect them to attend for the return that they get, particularly now we're a minority government in Lords terms. The expectation that they will turn up and stay for votes is excessive for people who have got careers outside or people who are retired and getting a bit frail. It's not reasonable, yet we do it. So in that sense, it's under-rewarded. In order to live you'd have to do something else or to have a decent pension. No other way of doing it.

Lord Whitty, Labour

I've not attended very much really in the last year but then I go through periods of attending quite a lot. The real reason that I'm not attending so much recently is because I'm struggling financially. I've got the bank on my back at the moment. We had a rather bad year last year. The country park wasn't ready enough for tourists and we didn't meet our target. I've got an overdraft and we've got to try and do something about it. So this year, I'm really budgeting everything very carefully and doing every bit of publicity that we possibly can now. So I'm really up in Scotland most of the time. That is more important to me than doing anything down here. But, if I was more relaxed up there and a little less worried about what's going on in Scotland, I would certainly come here more often.

Earl of Glasgow, Liberal Democrat

We were paid less than our Commons counterparts as ministers. But not that much less. Certain improvements were made over the last years. I can't object to the ministerial pay. In opposition, we only have our attendance allowance, but I have to say that it doesn't really cover the cost of keeping a separate establishment in London and all that. I'm commuting exactly like an MP. One of the joys of opposition is that I can get away earlier. As a minister Fridays were the days when you weren't confined to the House so you were off on some ministerial trip followed by a party function on Friday evening so you might not get back till Saturday morning. I do have to say the joy of opposition is that I will be back home tonight in good time. Last week I went back on Thursday morning. If I hadn't had business, I could have got away on Wednesday evening. It'll vary.

Lord Henley, Conservative

The downside of being a minister is definitely the situation of being locked in the chamber from 3.30 normally every afternoon. And here until midnight, what have you. That takes away from the satisfactions of being a minister but for me as Minister for Agriculture, where I'm Minister for the Regions, one of my main jobs is to go and visit agriculture in the regions. It's quite dreadful that I can't do that. I can't get off on visits because I'm stuck in here. So that is a downside but it has plusses. I've enjoyed the presidency, being the

Minister at the Agricultural Council in Brussels. And there again you have debates on those issues here. We have quite serious debates on CAP reform, the beef ban, and all of those kind of things. You get people here with enormous knowledge. I was advised when I first came in, do not speak on anything unless you know quite a lot about it, because there will always be a lot of people here who do know a lot about it. If you don't they'll know you don't. When I was energy spokesman, there were always former chairmen of BP and Shell, and Chairmen of Electricity Boards and British Gas and they really knew a great deal. On agriculture I face the mass ranks of the Tory farmers and landowners who've all been in it all their lives and so when it comes to detail they know what they're talking about. One has to treat them with respect. I would never take them on in an adversarial way, because I'd be bound to lose on the factual detail.

Lord Donoughue, Labour

When we were in opposition the Lords didn't have anything to do much until Christmas then it began to get tighter and tighter. Then in the Trinity Term it was very tight and you may be up three or four days a week, but in those days it depended upon the number of amendments we put down and whether we were going to try and beat the Government and that dictated the pace. So that in fact over the whole year I would say I was probably in on two days a week but it was much denser at the end of the year than it was at the beginning. All our contested business comes from the other end, so we don't get much after the Queen's Speech do we? But towards the end of the year when stuff's piling in, in the old days - and it would be the same now - the House of Lords starts off by meeting two or three days a week, then it meets four days a week. By the time we get to July we're meeting five days a week. So the load is much heavier.

Lord McCarthy, Labour

It's an odd atmosphere in a way, because the House of Lords has a lot less power. So there's no ambition. That is one of the of the strangest feelings about the place because you take on work, or you're given work by the whips, but you don't get paid any more for it. So you can work on a bill for months and months, full-time, and it'll take up your life, but you volunteered to do it, so you do it. You do find a lot of people who are overworked but, because it falls within their field, they try and champion a cause.

Lord Redesdale, Liberal Democrat

I've been here as a member for 20 years. I was always quite a regular attendee for the last eight years. Until 1st May I was a minister so I was here full-time. Since 1st May, I have been on the front bench, first shadowing my old Department of Education and Employment and since October, shadowing Home Affairs. Obviously, in opposition one can take a more relaxed view about the amount of time you're here, but I'm still here I suppose most days.

Lord Henley, Conservative

Monday I pick and bunch my flowers that I'm going to take down, and I sort out all the letters I'm going to take down and all the papers and everything else. Then my husband drives me to the airport, and we have a little time talking, and I fly down from Edinburgh. It takes an hour to get to Edinburgh, and then about an hour's flight from Edinburgh, and then about an hour or so to come up. Then I come up here, do my flowers and rush in to the chamber and start dealing with the post and the letters and all that.

Monday, Tuesday, Wednesday, Thursday. The House only sits four days, so it depends what's happening on Thursday if I can get away Thursday night. It may well be Friday morning. But there's quite a good 6.55 plane in the morning and I'm home at nine o'clock. So that gives me time to do all the things I need to do at home, work through the post and everything else.

I work through the letters, I see the dogs, get my hair done for another week, stock up with food for my husband, do some cooking, race round the garden, do all the flowers in the house and well, you know, just enjoy myself.

Lady Strange, Conservative

I don't find life in the Lords of financial benefit. In fact the extent of the payment allowances that we get is sufficient for a bare standard of life, and a very bare one at that. You can't make money out of it in the real sense. So there is a financial disadvantage and you do need a certain amount of outside income which I, fortunately, do have as a result of my practise, to be able to sustain you in a reasonably tolerable but not luxurious standard of life. It's surprising how many members of the Lords do have outside interests. Not all of them are completely without resources. Even on our side they do have the odd job for the union and so on, and I think that by and large they are able to manage on it. You don't find them getting drunk in the bar or anything like that. You may get an occasional one that's the worse for wear but they're known anyway - and were known from their Commons days. It's not a life I would choose to make a living out of. But the difficulty for me is that I believe in things.

Lord Bruce, Labour

There's an enormous difference in being in power. I didn't get the job I wanted. I was missed altogether. I was rescued to be deputy chief whip. He doesn't do any real political work and he didn't really do any whipping work, because the ordinary whips do that. So the deputy chief whip is paid more than an ordinary whip but has nothing whatsoever to do. I said that I should have something as a condition, first of all to Ivor Richard and then to Tony Blair. So because there aren't enough Lords ministers to go round I do an enormous amount of parliamentary business. I'm on my feet nearly every day.

I'm not doing departmental responsibilities as well, and because they know I'm covering a range of departments, I always get written briefing material. I always have a briefing meeting, and the result is I probably get better briefing than people who are working in a very great hurry. I'm not paid by the departments I work for. I'm paid at a parliamentary secretary's level. Lords ministers are very badly paid. They lost out on the last round. They had to get the senior salary review body to report very quickly and they couldn't finish doing the Lords ministers' salaries. So we're still paid on the previous round basis and we get about 60 or 70 per cent.

Lord McIntosh, Labour

The advantage that MPs have is that they have their constituents, they have their case work to deal with. Most of them do work assiduously at their case work so that must inform them in their parliamentary duties. We don't have that direct contact with people. So we've actually got to make an effort to ensure that we do keep in contact with the real world. Initially, when I first came into the House I had an ordinary job, I was an engineer working in industry. Then I got elected to the city council in Manchester and, at the same time, took redundancy from work. Being a member of the city council and being a member of the House of Lords I found very useful in the sense that the information that I have at this end, at Westminster, was helped by working on the council, and vice versa. The difficulty in trying to do two jobs 200 miles apart just became impossible. So I am at this moment attempting to become a councillor in London. I've moved to London, relocated my party and trade union membership down here, and I'm getting plumbed into the local community.

Lord Monkswell, Labour

It's very hard work without a secretary because you've got to open your own post, reply to your own letters as far as you can and you have to pay your own postage. Although there is a secretarial allowance its not very much, so that you have to not only do your own work but secretarial work as well, and it is extremely difficult. On the other hand, in the House of Lords fortunately you don't have constituents so that a good deal of the work they have to do in the House of Commons doesn't have to be done in the Lords. They write to the House of Lords but they don't necessarily expect a reply. Over the Firearms Bill the Labour Party had misunderstood the public mood and I had hundreds of letters from decent people. There was no way that I could reply to those letters without secretarial help and at the same time spend hours opposing the Bill. Indeed in the last analysis I tried to rally the House of Lords, and those peers who passed the very good amendments, to insist on the amendments and I forced the House to a division, something which I think hasn't been done for a very long time. Unfortunately they gave in.

Lord Stoddart, Labour

I've been here pretty frequently since I inherited. Of course, it's been influenced by the fact that the process which began in '88 has, in my view, led to the collapse of British universities. The reduction in unit costs is beginning to make serious university education impossible. I've come in here, at the moment precisely when I was losing faith in my old career. So it struck me at precisely the moment when I was really looking for a second vocation and I've been bloody lucky. Now it looks as though I may be losing the second vocation as well. It's like having two horses shot under you in a battle.

My attendance depends what the business is and it depends whether they're bowling at my wicket. Tom Strathclyde, when he was government Chief Whip, once replied, "Whichever wicket I'm bowling at, you always seem to be standing at it". The trouble is once involved in an issue, one gets the briefs on it forever after. Obviously I got involved with everything to do with higher education, and for a while higher education bills were as frequent as local government bills or trade union bills in the first half of the Thatcher period. Then I got the Social Security brief at precisely the moment when it became really active. Then I started getting involved in things like the gay rights issue and trying to put a stop to Michael Howard, or should I say Michael Straw?

Lord Russell, Liberal Democrat

I attend about 99% of the time, all days. Particularly since I left the European Parliament I've sought to keep up to date with everything that goes on inside the European Community. That means that I have to come in even during the recess to look at the latest EEC nonsense put out by the Commission. It's now coming in in great dollops of it, most of which won't be read by ministers because EEC documents are very rarely read by ministers.

I was a member of the European Parliament while I was a member of the House of Lords. I'm never quite sure whether they sent me to get me out of the way, or whether they sent me because they thought I could do a good job. But once again, being there I made it a point to enjoy what I was doing, and tackling it as best I could.

Stoddard and myself, we've got about 70 supporters now in the House of Lords, including a few on our own benches who, while supportive, don't like to be overtly supporting. They put a very great store on party loyalty and don't like putting themselves in the position where they criticise the party line. It's not because they're cowardly or anything of that kind, it's just because that's their interpretation of what party loyalty really means.

Lord Bruce, Labour

I don't find it difficult to speak because I did actually train as an actress all those years ago, in another generation. Being a cross-bencher, I don't get any help with research and background. I've got to do all that myself. You don't get to speak when you want if it's a starred question and you want to have a quick fire from 2.30 to 3.00, on a subject because it goes Labour, Conservative, Liberal Democrat, and then cross-benchers, so we're always fourth. So if you miss the first round, that's four gone, then it comes back to eight, and it all depends on the length of the question and the length of the reply and for half an hour you've got four starred questions, so that's seven minutes per question. It's not an awful lot. So you can miss out on that.

At the moment, it's terribly hard to get a seat in the chamber so most people hobble round in the Prince's chamber. Unless you're directly involved you can't sit anywhere. At committee stage, obviously it goes in turn. If a Conservative gets up, because if he's pushing the amendment then the Under-Secretary answers and then normally it would go back to the government's own benches, then the Liberal Democrats. They try as far as is possible to have a kind of order. There, you can just sit, leap up and sit down. But nobody does a Dennis Skinner.

In debates you put your name down in the government whip's office. You've got a written speakers' list so you can time it. If there are more than 25 speakers, apart from the minister opening and answering and then the two opposition spokesmen, plus the government, twice as much say twenty minutes, ten for the other two, then if there are more than twenty-five, you might be limited to five minutes, or six.

The debates by and large tend to be timed. That's if the debate's put down by a peer. If they're on an issue like a select committee report, then it's an unlimited debate so that can go on for five or six hours. Then the length of speeches is unlimited, but everybody's listening power isn't. If it drones on you see them all going.

Lady Wharton, Cross-bencher

We do have to produce big turnouts slightly more often than the big parties do. On the other hand I've always found the party absolutely and entirely reasonable about academic commitments. On occasion, I've brought tutorials to the House and had them in this interview room here when there's a big whip. The college is only 20 minutes away down the Strand. My record is teaching in college at 3 and on my feet in the House at 3.30. So I can do things I couldn't possibly do if I came from Oxford or Cambridge. That helps. But because the party knows that I always will be here if I possibly can, if I tell them I can't be here, they accept it without a murmur. And that's the way a relationship of trust works.

Lord Russell, Liberal Democrat

When I came here I carried on doing some part-time academic work, partly to get an income. I just taught on Fridays. Plus Saturdays and Sundays which is actually when I wrote the speeches and amendments. I was doing six days a week. I went home, I taught and just kept a small income going that way.

The real drawback of this place was that I was living off savings. My total income in opposition, after you took out the Housing allowance, was about £7000 to live on for the entire year. Now that was slightly less than social security rates. And out of that you had to pay all your food, clothes, most of your travel expenses like taxis, all your books and postage stamps. I had something like 400 letters on pension splitting and I had to reply to everyone by hand and buy the postage stamps. That's how under-resourced it is. It was really hard work. The main difference obviously going into government is all the support networks and services. But what it isn't is a part-time voluntary House.

Lady Hollis, Labour

I love it. It's a bugger living in Oxford because they ring you up and say that you've got a vote tomorrow and I say, "Well, I can't come". It's a bugger being an academic in the sense that with an academic everything is in the diary for months ahead. So somewhere in Manchester there's a little group of 15 people who are confidently sitting there expecting you to come through the door at half past ten because they'd written to you nine months previously. That's laid out and I can't fit that together with the kind of instant movement of this place where you never know until Thursday what's coming on next week. Everybody down the other end will put the demands of the whip as their first call, and that's the way they think we're going to be up here. If you live in London you can do that but if you live in Oxford it's a bugger. I take the view if you're attending a conference or something you can duck it, but if you're performing you can't.

Lord McCarthy, Labour

When I was Leader of the House of Lords, I always took the view that, if your opinion is asked, you should give it honestly. There is absolutely no point in saying it's perfectly all right when it isn't going to be. So I always said so. It wasn't - as you can imagine - a very popular voice, or happily received. But in fact, without wishing to blow my own trumpet, I was nearly always right on these matters. You can tell when you're here, what you can get through and what you can't. I often used to say to my colleagues, "I'll put that up but I can tell you you're not going to get it through." "Why won't you get it through?" "Well, it's to do with the disabled and I can tell you that there's somebody like Lady Masham in a wheelchair sitting there. She will put the opposite side of the case. She will get a lot of sympathy, and who knows, she's probably right, and it will stack up the cross-benchers and the Labour opposition and some of our own supporters and you'll lose." The numbers will be like that. And almost invariably on those occasions, we did lose.

Lady Young, Conservative

The officials and the ministers in the Commons treated me very badly. They didn't tell me a thing. Not a thing. Eventually, I had a showdown about it, because my predecessor complained of the same thing. I have to do statements. I'd never seen them, never been told they were going to happen. It was really bad. They just didn't think I existed, actually.

Lady Trumpington, Conservative

We've seven whips myself included and 14 ministers, four or five of whom are ministers of state. Parliamentary secretaries even in the Commons are not very highly regarded by various departments, so you wouldn't expect a vast deference from the civil service. But, in general, I haven't found the civil service too difficult in recognising that there is an important Lords stage, particularly when they've got legislation. Cabinet ministers, even in the Commons, say, "Well, we've dealt with that." I do regard the Lords as important. Whether from the point of view of the political and legislative processes, it should be as important, I'm not at all sure. I think mirroring the Commons procedures doesn't really necessarily improve the quality of legislation. As far as the input from the ministers is concerned, they're very heavily briefed. Lords are quite often more probing than the Commons, and more tenacious, and because it's all done on the floor of the House you have to perform reasonably well. If you've got a majority in the Committees in the House of Commons by and large you only have to sit there and get the vote through.

Lord Whitty, Labour

There is bred into every member of the House of Commons a contempt for the House of Lords. They always think - particularly Tory ministers in the House of Commons - that their House of Lords` colleagues are one: very stupid, two: unversed in the ways of the world and three: completely ignorant about politics. Therefore they are there because somebody has to take the stuff through the House of Lords but you don't give them much to do in the department. Some idle Lords ministers say, "Fine". Some who have been in the House of Commons say, "Come on pull the other one". They actually show they know what's what. Others, I hope I was one, say "Well, I haven't become a minister just to be trampled on. I want to fight my corner. I want to be clear what I'm responsible for. And I'm bloody well going to do it." You have much more fun that way.

Lord Cranborne, Conservative

I've never worked so hard in my life. I loved it. I absolutely loved it. I saw the most incredible things and I gained a huge impression of how wonderful people were who worked all over the country in the Health Service. I took a very big Social Security bill through and at the end of it I had all the civil servants, 21 of them, into the guest room. I bought them all Pimms and somebody came rushing down the corridor and said, the Prime Minister wants to see you. You can imagine I was absolutely terrified. So I went. Willy Whitelaw was Leader, and there was Margaret who I was terrified of, and she had had a few drinks before I came in. I said, "Willy has been the most wonderful help to me" and she said, "You're not so bad yourself old girl". And clapped me on the back.

For the first year and a half, I was in charge of Aids. Nobody else wanted to touch it. I was going all over the country shaking hands long before it was the thing to do. I was responsible for Mental Health, which is a very tricky subject. The love of my life was being Minister for War Pensioners. They were quite a tricky old lot but you've got to talk straight to them. So I really loved that. But it was, give us this day, our daily Trumpington, from the dispatch box. And boy oh boy did I suffer. When I first was answering questions, I was hopeless at it. I never could find the right answer. Everything was written down. And the Opposition used to shout at me, try number 45, try 51 and the sweat would pour off me.

The Opposition whip in the Lords came to me and she said, "We girls should stick together. Come with me". She said, "I've kept one of my folders and I'll show you how I did it. It may help you to find the right supplementary". She'd got little stickers in little colours that she'd done, and I copied that and from the moment on I was all right. But they all used to mock my bits of paper that stuck out, all different colours.

Lady Trumpington, Conservative

Instinctively the civil servants say the House of Lords doesn't matter. I don't know what the civil servants thought of me but I thought I was on the whole extremely well-served. If you insisted and you knew what you wanted after the initial misunderstanding, you got very good service indeed. It's like the rest of the world, you've got the earn your respect haven't you? But the other thing that I do notice is that great Secretaries of State are slower to learn. One Secretary of State who I think should remain nameless, rang me up one day and said, "I've got this very complicated bill coming your way, Lord Ferrers is taking it through. He's a wonderful man and all that but do you think he's able to?" So I said to him, "I'd like to tell you two things. One, the only man who has a chance of getting this bill through the House of Lords is Lord Ferrers. Secondly, his favourite occupation in life, and remember he's been a minister for 30 years, is pretending he's an idiot because he thinks it's very funny. Let me tell you he's not an idiot. I promise you he understands this bill. Completely". There were certain things in the bill that were completely out but he just bullshitted his way through and made them laugh. As a result they forgot to look at some of the detail. It does rather show that these great Secretaries of State don't understand us at all.

Lord Cranborne, Conservative

As far as the civil servants were concerned, I don't think they treated one any differently, better or worse, than any other minister. I think some of them, Commons backbenchers and for that matter Commons ministers, tend to look askance at Lords ministers, partly because they don't understand the pressures we operate under. It's different. We have to answer for the whole department, we don't have constituency responsibilities. It's a different way of doing it. We do operate in a House of Commons-centred system. There is a kind of presumption that someone like me is where he is because he couldn't hack it to get through to the House of Commons. I don't think that's true but you've just got to get on with it and show them you're good enough.

Lord Inglewood, Conservative

It's politics, not power, in the Lords. There isn't the power that one can have in the Commons, but I did have chance to be a minister for eight years in a range of different departments. Even as junior minister you have a degree of power which gets greater when you move up to be a Minister of State rather than a parliamentary under-secretary. Doing that, you have the chance to influence policy developments. What power one has in opposition is another matter, but someone's got to be there to argue the case so that government legislation is properly tested.

Lord Henley, Conservative

I sometimes feel like I'm 500 miles from the other end. I've worked quite hard, as an individual, trying to maintain relationships down the other end. I go to virtually all the PLP meetings. I was Vice-Chair of the women's group which runs across both Houses. I've got quite a number of good friends down the other end and I try and stay in contact with them. So I regard myself as a Labour Party activist in Parliament first and only second as in the Lords I try very hard but it is very difficult. On social security, they're always surprised when I say, "I may have some difficulty with this. Do you really want me to be defeated on this major issue associated with lone parents and you have it back in the Commons?" "Well, no actually". "Well, in that case, these are the areas I'm waiting to negotiate on, concede on, come back for the government amendment, whatever".

Lady Hollis, Labour

My worst memory is when I was briefly on the Opposition front bench. I was number two to Peter Carrington on Foreign Affairs. That was fine but then I was Opposition spokesman on Transport and I was probably the only member of the House who couldn't drive a car so I didn't find those debates easy. But the worst moments came at the very beginning. I was, very controversially, made a minister for the government. It was a monstrous act of nepotism on the part of my uncle by marriage, Harold Macmillan, to make me a minister and he'd no justification for doing it. I was thrown in at the deep end by the first debate at which I spoke from the despatch box which was on Rhodesia. It was not easy. Quintin, who was leader, was very apprehensive and I was sure I'd make a frightful hash of it because I had to open the debate. It went off pretty well and Duncan Sandys, my boss, who had been very critical of my appointment, came down and sat on the steps of the throne for my speech and wrote me a very nice note afterwards and he accepted me. So that first debate was vital and important, and I managed not to make too much of a mess of it. It helped the next four years very much.

Duke of Devonshire, Cross-bencher

I was very sad to hand over as Leader. But we all know in politics the way the cookie crumbles, and Willie wanted to come to the Lords and Margaret Thatcher wanted him to be leader and Willie wanted to be leader. I think that he was a very good leader of the House of Lords. He was always very good to me personally, and I gave him my support. You have the good times, you have the bad times. It's no use going on for a long whinge about things. It doesn't get you anywhere.

I've had a very good run for my money, I actually went to the Foreign Office and had the most extraordinarily interesting time. I'd travelled very little, brought up the family and practically done a full-time job, so the amount of time you've got for foreign travel is very limited. So I said, "Put me down for foreign travel". I saw the world, and an enormous number of extremely interesting people.

Lady Young, Conservative

In '92 I was 58. That's quite retired. But what I knew was that if I didn't take politics and government seriously then, it was over. I felt if I was to have any hope of being a minister, I had to work seriously at it. It takes a while to learn the House, because it's a very special style which some people get wrong. Ex-Commons MPs rarely succeed in the Lords. They're usually too aggressive or too adversarial, and point-scoring. If you don't come from the Commons, on the whole you haven't a style at all. So you need to develop that.

I spent some time at the dispatch box, trying to learn the best way of doing it. Everyone has their own style. For instance for Questions I never use a note. I'd decided early on, I gave my maiden speech without a note, and certainly for Questions, and even though answering as a minister, I read the opening but I never use a note after that. I think it's the only way to answer a question. Usually what people read out is some blunderbuss, that doesn't answer the question at all. In opposition I got frustrated with that, so I decided I would always try and answer the question. When you're doing a speech, you have to be more careful, and read it out.

I decided not to be adversarial and not to try and score party points, because my observation here is it makes no difference. Nobody here's running for election. Nobody here so far has been thrown out. Nobody here gets reported in the media. So what's the point? You get people come in here who fight old party battles. It just washes over their heads. Peers will walk out. Whereas if you're trying to make reasonable points, you will normally have quite a reasonable audience here, and people will listen. The attendance is usually greater than in the Commons. And there is a dialogue. You make points and people come back. They will not shout "yah-boo". They will question your facts or ask if the answer is quite right. That's quite a satisfying process.

Lord Donoughue, Labour

Being a government backbencher isn't as much fun as being an opposition bachbencher but being of ministerial rank and having ministerial responsibilities is enormous fun. I do get things changed. I'm part of the ministerial team and decisions are taken collectively. Chris Smith is the kind of person who listens to other people and we argue things out. It's great. I follow the line that's given but it's my own words all the time. I use my own words, even from the Foreign Office. I'm a bit cautious with the Treasury but that's true of all ministers whether from the Commons or the Lords. You know that in the Foreign Office if you say the wrong thing the war will break out. So you've got to be a bit careful.

Lord McIntosh, Labour

One of the characteristics of political activity is a lot of it's to do with dealing with people and lining up an argument you wish to see advanced in a way which is likely to be most effective. Unless you understand the conventions and you know the people, it's a great deal more difficult. The most difficult thing of all was going to Cabinet Committees, sitting round a table with a lot of people who had worked together as House of Commons members, had known each other well for longish numbers of years, and I didn't know how their minds worked. They didn't have any idea about me, and I assumed they thought, "Who on earth is this young chap who's suddenly been parachuted in from somewhere else?".

I think one of the problems for the House of Commons is that it has become extremely introverted as an institution, and politics seems to me to be perceived by members of the House of Commons, to be about the House of Commons. Almost to the exclusion of everything else. I think that's very unhealthy.

Lord Inglewood, Conservative

Those few people who've experienced it in both Houses, John MacKay as an example, will point out that you can't get away with the "yah-boo sucks" type of responses that a lot of ministers have always have got away with in the Commons. You are expected to answer, and particularly if you're a relatively junior minister you cannot get away with being rude to the great and the good. When a former Prime Minister like Lord Callagham or Lady Thatcher intervenes, the House expects you to give them a proper response. An adequate response will not go down well. So from that point of view, it can be tougher. The other thing about questions here is that, in the Commons, they come up just once a month. Here, there are four questions down every day, those questions last up to a maximum of half an hour. You have no idea what questions are going to go down. It just depends on what moves them.

Our duties are much wider. I have to cover the whole department. One day

I'm talking about Fisheries, next day on B6, beef on the bone, agriculture policy, milk quotas, flood defences. As a Lords minister you work on a wider field. So I would say if you take that and the amount of time you have to be in the chamber, we probably work harder than the ministers in the Commons but are less regarded by the department. That has to be fought.

The department's views was that Lords` ministers didn't matter, because it was quite clear that under the Tories, Lords ministers didn't matter. People of my department and other departments have told us they just got them to answer the odd question, reading out the brief and that was basically that. They were mainly hereditary ministers with no great background. Most of us have been in politics all our lives and we're not going to be treated that way. So each of us, in our own way, have to establish in the department that we want to be taken seriously. For me it meant some months insisting I received copies of papers, because they wouldn't automatically copy me papers. A lot depends on who your top minister is. I'm very lucky because Jack Cunningham is superb as a department minister, he's totally inclusive. That was very helpful. He just insisted I be included. I insisted. On one or two occasions on important subjects where civil servants didn't copy me the important minutes, I even wrote to them personally, and gave them a rocket. That's all resolved now. I think the other ministers I know, Tessa Blackstone, Margaret Jay they are all treated totally as a proper minister. But in most areas we had to fight to achieve that.

Lord Donoughue, Labour

Questions are in some ways more difficult than in your House for two reasons. One, they go on for longer, the question and answer is not restricted to one question, or even two, for a former defence minister and his colleagues were leaping up and down asking rather persistent but polite questions, as well as the Former Chief of Defence Staff - and he does know his onions so shouting a bit won't do.

You quickly realise that the House of Lords at its worst is ghastly, but in the House of Lords at its best the minister does have to know his stuff. So you bloody well read your papers. And you know what the arguments are and if you don't, something I knew as Leader is ,if your frontbench isn't up to it, they bloody well come and tell you. And it's intimated that it would be a good idea if you dropped them.

Lord Cranborne, Conservative

Departments don't always have to have a peer. There are always a number of departments that don't have ministers. For example, I think only twice this century, the Treasury had a minister in the Lords. Both John MacKay who I share this room with, and myself, have served as Treasury spokesmen. I must say, that's quite a difficult role because acting as a spokesman for a department you're not in means you're very much more dependent on the officials than you would be if you are there as minister yourself. But I think as a minister in the department, you will have the influence you yourself can bring to bear. And I imagine there are some who've probably had relatively little influence because they didn't exert themselves. But I'm sure that I did have proper influence and when I became a Minister of State I don't believe I was a mere token minister of state within the Department of Education and Employment. I was an exact equal of my counterpart, Eric Forth. He had his responsibilities and I had mine.

The difficulties for a Lords minister is the fact that you're representing the whole of the department when it comes to legislation or debates or whatever, going through the House. You do find that there are times when you're spending much more time in the House than your counterparts in the Commons. I never had a particularly heavy legislative burden in any of the departments I was in. But if, for example, you take someone like, Derek Williams of Mostyn, in the Home Office at the moment, my guess is with the six or so Home Office Bills going through this year, he actually won't find much time for departmental work. On top of that, I think he's also having to do the Welsh Bill because there isn't a Welsh Minister in the Lords. So you can find yourself doing a lot more parliamentary work than your Commons counterparts. You obviously have to have a grasp over the whole of the department, because questions can come up on all subjects, and it's slightly harder when you're speaking for another department. It's also slightly harder speaking for parts of departments that aren't your own. When you get something on your own departmental responsibilities, you always feel in a much stronger position.

Lord Henley, Conservative

I attended the House of Lords more and more, and then Harold Wilson put me in the Government after I'd been in the House for six years. That made me feel very happy indeed. We had multiple coverage of posts in the House of Lords to what now seems a ridiculous degree. At one time I was doing work which was done by 11 ministers in the House of Commons - it was only for three months but still I'll never forget that time. I was actually doing the Ministry of Housing and Local Government and I was speaking also for the Minster of Technology (Tony Benn) and Social Security and Health (for Crossman). I did have to become a full time attender - with the odd pillow in the corridor - because anything can come with Social Security. The Tory majority was mobilised to defeat the government at that time. As Tory opposition, they defeated us whenever they wanted. It was about the same as it is now, a little bit less because the numbers are somewhat less than they were then. Which produced a Labour demand for reform. It rarely made life difficult. I remember a meeting of the Legislative Committee where they were really tearing their hair about the hold up and there was nothing to be done. But it didn't happen often.

Lord Kennet, Labour

I always found the extraordinary ignorance of departmental colleagues about the workings of the Lords. You get remarks such as "You mean you can have amendments at third reading?" or, if you suffered a defeat at committee stage, "Well, can't you just overturn that at report stage?" It might be possible in the Commons but certainly it`s completely outside the way we work. It`s ignorance. I mentioned about Question Time. We just have four questions any day on any subject, and again this would surprise any who hadn't bothered to look at this House. I always found Secretaries of State needed a defeat or two in the Lords before they managed to develop the right knack of dealing with legislation going through the Lords. One always wants to try to persuade your Secretary of State that there should be a few goodies to hand out in the Bill as it was going through. A few small concessions. You must have a concession or two to save for the Lords. A few concessions did vast amounts to oil the wheel of the legislative process in a way that if you tried to take a bill through without any amendments at all, you were sure to come unstuck.

Lord Henley, Conservative

There's a glass ceiling here. There's three or four Ministers of State and a dozen Parliamentary Under Secretaries and that's it really. Plus the Leader. People down the other end don't actually take the Lords seriously, do they? Until they suddenly realise, as now, that the Tory party's running a party across two Houses. In that sense I get slightly irritated by people's failure to understand what's going on in the Lords. We have a unicameral system, and add on the revising and debating chamber. At the moment and certainly when we were in opposition, it was this revising chamber which inflicted defeats on the government. There were no defeats down the other end except for VAT on fuel. I think that was the only one in five years. I was getting about eight a year and some of my colleagues were getting as many defeats on the government, some of which actually stood down the other end. Now in government, this is actually where the opposition is. Because they can outvote us any time. So it's a mistake to dismiss the role of the Lords.

Lady Hollis, Labour

I didn't have the backing here of a vast array of PPS's. If you take the Department of Education, you have five Commons ministers; there were two PPS's, there was a whip, there are an awful lot of people to start bringing in backbenchers to help. Here, one tries to manage with just the assistance of your whip. There are only a total of seven whips, who'll be covering a lot of other departments. What we try to do is find out who had interests in this particular bill and brief them where we felt we needed support. What I certainly did in government, and still do in opposition on any bill, is have a brief meeting, lasting about an hour, 12 o'clock on the day of any committee or report stage of a bill, just to run through what I think are the likely major issues that are going to be coming up and try to enlist support. Or if I think some of my natural supporters, or unnatural supporters, are not going to be supportive, deal with some of their concerns in advance.

Lord Henley, Conservative

It's difficult to get people into this place because they don't pay them very much. So you tend to be relying on either people of a certain age who may or may not know anything about the subject themselves, or young hereditary peers who are not necessarily always competent. And it did show from time to time. The last 18 months I would say the quality improved but for a few years before that it was dire.

Lord Tordoff, Liberal Democrat

You'll know the famous story of the brief that was headed 'Not a very good brief but this'll do for the Lordships on a quiet day'. I didn't actually ever see any evidence of that. There were occasions when one had a sneaking suspicion that departments weren't providing as strong a brief for the Lords as they were for the Commons. It's something that all the Leaders of the Lords that I served under were pretty firm about, and if they heard instances, they wanted to know why it was happening. They always wanted to make sure that,with any legislation, the same bill team took the bill through both the Lords and the Commons. There could be occasions when a statement was being repeated in this House, where you couldn't have the same backup as the Commons, because the principle backup was going to the Secretary of State in the Commons. But in the main, the service I got was pretty good. I can remember one or two occasions doubling up for someone else who happened to be away, or speaking for a department that didn't have a minister. There were occasions when I think the service one got wasn't necessarily as good as it ought to be. I can think of an incident going right back to when I was in the Whip's Office, in dealing with a question for education where I did get into considerable difficulties and I think it was largely because the officials didn't brief me properly.

Lord Henley, Conservative

We've got some very fine prodders who were very good in their area, most of them are all Commons men really, and they'd prod and prod, and push and push, and they get the other lot prodding back. But it's so easy for ministers, in their elegance and superiority, to say "I'll write to you". They didn't care. The most outstanding example of this was a very attractive old bird, Lady Trumpington, Conservative. I once heard her say in answer to a very fine question which had nailed her right into a corner: "The answer to that is poof". That's very extreme, but the House rocked with laughter. But she was like that. She didn't care and it didn't really matter.

Your whole political career is not dependent upon your making a good reply. In the Commons, if you're a minister and you get up and make a total bloody cod's arse, if you do that twice you're for the chop. I think it's very dangerous for anybody, however eminent, who makes a complete cod's arse three or four times in a row at the dispatch box because his days are numbered. But in the Lords it doesn't matter. I've seen old Ferrers answer a debate and get to the end of what he's got, and he just kind of smiles and mumbles. They don't care. We don't quite think we can do that and I think our Leader wouldn't like it if we did. But some of them got away with murder.

Lord McCarthy, Labour

One of my first thoughts listening to a lot of junior ministers, was to understand what Presbyterians meant when they complained about a reading ministry. A junior minister doesn't have very much authority. On the other hand, you get some junior ministers, particularly some in the present Government, who are of absolutely first class ability and know their subjects inside out. They have some authority inside government because they actually talk sense. And the names of Patricia Hollis and Gareth Williams come to mind. A lot of the ministers in the Lords are absolutely top flight and Helene Heyman and Margaret Jay are top flight as well. I had a little exchange with Gary five minutes ago. There was a question on the Millennium Dome. I asked, "Had the minister got the message from the latest Wonder Bra advertisement, Some Domes Enjoy Public Support.?" As soon as I was out of the chamber, Gary said, "Thank you for your uplifting question".

Lord Russell, Liberal Democrat

I prepare all my stuff. We're in the 20th century, for heavens sake. We've got lap tops, we've got e-mails, we've got an excellent library, and the computer room is so good, it's helpful. I'm more efficient working here than I think I've ever been anywhere else. The ability of the staff to produce the things and to give you the service is so much better than anywhere else. I've been managing director of businesses and you ask for information, and you'll get it three days later and you have to thump and bash and really go mad. Here you go down to the library and you say, "I've got a feeling about eighteen months ago there was something about such and such" and, "Oh yes, milady, yes, we'll look for it," and within minutes you'll get it. You get all the information you require, the courtesy, the respect, the willingness. Yet although they dress like Black Rod in strange gear as the kids would say, deep down, all these people just want to serve the Palace of Westminster and the members. Never in my whole life have I met with such courtesy in a dignified way, and that really is very exhilarating. If you're surrounded by good things, by good people, you actually give of your best. If you work in sloppy portacabins surrounded by nasty, sloppy people, you don't. You know, part of you resents it. Whereas here, you come in and the atmosphere is such that it encourages you to give of your best.

Lady O'Cathain, Conservative

I was on the front bench from 1979 to 1990 dealing with treasury matters, therefore with economic and trade matters, until my stance on Europe became a little embarrassing to party hierarchy which suddenly switched over from being highly sceptical about Europe to being more supportive. It was put to me in 1990 or thereabout that there would shortly be a change of government.

Therefore, we would have to bring in younger peers to begin to have experience of the front bench and some of us older ones might think it right to give them some experience. I thought it was a very good thing. So I immediately consented.

When we reassembled for the new session I suddenly found that in spite of the age of a number of my colleagues I was the only one who'd 'volunteered' to step down. I therefore put two and two together because at the same time it was also made clear from other quarters that my attitude towards the Common Market was becoming a little embarrassing for the party leadership and so they didn't prevent it.

For my own part I felt a profound sense of liberation because the physical fact of not having a despatch box to rest your papers was more than compensated for by the freedom of speech which I rediscovered.

Lord Bruce, Labour

There are a whole range of things that are enjoyable about the House of Lords. One is having friendly companionship and good colleagues; another is being able to raise issues of the day, although I'm finding like a lot of my colleagues that being in government is rather different from being in opposition. Being in opposition is so easy because it's easier and more fun and you can attack. Now we're in government it's rather different. One has got to take questions and queries, especially significant ones, to government ministers behind the scenes rather than up front - at least that's the way I feel it should be done - we've all got to be playing as part of the same team.

Lord Monkswell, Labour

I take it all very seriously. Because the House takes us seriously actually and watches us. We're all dressed up. We sit down there like penguins. We're only guys that are dressed up, we're pretty obvious and they actually note what you say and they note how you vote. This is the alarming thing. I've had two brushes with whips in the Lords for voting for Labour and not for voting for the Conservative Government. It was a Tory whip and I gripped him and I told him we were independent. When I was brought in here and we had our little induction course which they very kindly ran for us we were told that we were here for ourselves. We were here because we were cross-benchers. We're traditionally cross-benchers although we sit on the government side. But we're here in a way for ourselves and I regard myself here as an independent moral Christian voice as far as I can be under the very complex issues which Parliament faces. I think many of the Lords actually look to us for this and expect and hope that we will contribute. I've never felt on probation and I've never felt that actually what I tried to say wasn't listened to in a very courteous and thoughtful way. It's much easier speaking here than the General Synod and it's a much more friendly and supportive gathering of people.

Bishop of Lincoln

The great thing is if you want to work in the House of Lords, there's work to be done. People who say there's nothing to do, it's because they're not looking. I had my great interest in the Co-op and retailing so there were people outside the House who wanted me to do things. I have to earn a living, because when you come from the Commons at the age of 58, your pension is frozen 'til you're 65. Whilst the allowances are neither generous nor ungenerous, I need to earn a living. So I built up a small dossier of people who wanted me to work for them; the Co-op, principally. I worked for the Co-op Bank, Co-op Travel and Co-op Insurance, and the Head officer of the Prison Officers' Association is in Edmonton, so David Evans, the General Secretary, said we need someone in the House of Lords, in Parliament. So I represent the Prison Officers'. In my time in the Lords, I've visited 32 prisons. I've enjoyed my time, and I'm still enjoying it.

Lord Graham, Labour

I don't have to come more than I want to. I come once a day every day. I went to three prisons last week and you can't do that if you're stuck in the Commons. On the whole, I wouldn't have been a good Commons man. I have a great advantage in coming and speaking here. No doubt about it it's limited. You're not going to upset the whole nation by what we say, but it's a good opportunity. If you're a backbencher it's the same old place. Not only a club but a bit of a hospital.

Lord Longford, Labour

I enjoy it enormously. It's a bit of a lotus land for somebody like me. It's much easier being down here and enjoying it all than actually dealing with day to day hassle and problems in the diocese of Lincoln really. I wouldn't say its an escape from reality; it's an escape to another kind of reality. I think that's how I look at it. Its easier and you can escape into it and I have to watch, I try and discipline myself, as I have to do all the time as a Bishop, in the use of time where you put yourself to the best advantage.

Bishop of Lincoln

It kept me involved in politics on a daily active basis. And occasionally you had a bit of sun - the odd victory. It keeps you young. The other thing about this place - the reason that people last so long is that they're engaged. Their minds are engaged and they've got something to get on with. We do get some amazing people really. Still remain bright and cheerful until their 90's.

Lord Tordoff, Liberal Democrat

Once you inherit these titles and it enables you to get involved with legislative procedures down in Westminster, you might as well get in and do it. If you're allowed to do it, go down there and do it. Politics have always been involved with dentistry, and I suddenly thought now I can actually help with this because I can speak from personal experience. I got involved in the mid 70s, and I work with the various dental unions and do what I can on behalf of dentists and other things that I do.

Lord Colwyn, Conservative

I enjoy it. And on top of that, I have had eight years in government. Having had the privilege of that, one does have a duty to go on for a while in opposition. How long I shall go on doing it is another matter. I think one of the other problems of a Lords career is there is something of a glass ceiling. You can only go so far. I got to the stage of being a Minister of State in one of the bigger departments. There aren't many other jobs beyond that in government, and I wouldn't want to, as it were, move sideways to a less prestigious department or whatever. So, should we have won the last election - which in retrospect, looked unlikely - I probably wouldn't have been staying on for more than a couple of years, and then going off to do other things and spending more time with my family.

Lord Henley, Conservative

I think it's an enormous privilege to be in Parliament. The height of my ambition was reached when I walked through St. Stephen's entrance. I am fortunate in not having any ambition. I was chuffed to be a Member of Parliament. Everything that's happened to me since has just come along. I've never sought anything. I've never asked for anything for myself either. I think an ambition to do a good job, that's a perfectly worthy ambition, but it's a great privilege to be an elected Member of the House of Commons and a very great privilege to come up here because one's able to participate in the government of the country.

Lord Weatherill,   Cross-bencher

I became President of the War Widows, which I'm very proud of because I love them all desperately - they are lovely ladies, and I think, I hope that I have helped them in some ways to bring up their image. It's rather nice that there is somebody somewhere who can have a voice for you if you haven't got a voice yourself.

Lady Strange,   Conservative

There are two things against standing for Parliament. One is the way you have to sell yourself in order to get the selection in the first place, which I find difficult, within the party mainly. The other is, it's much nicer being a back-bencher in the Lords than in the Commons and this must be even more so if you're 40. Unless you're a minister in the Commons it is a really boring life; a life for which you have great expectations. But you have no influence what-soever until you've got a government position. That would have taken 18 years had I gone into the Commons at nearly 40. I'm 55 now. If I'd gone in at 40, 15 years of opposition would have been dreadful.

Lord Whitty,   Labour

When I was in opposition, one year we had four Social Security Bills, includ-ing the Disability Bill, and I could win amendments here that we hadn't a hope in hell of winning down the Commons. You could never get a a victo-ry in the Commons or defeat the government. The trick up here was not only to get the victory but to get enough Tories attached to your numbers so it wasn't overturned down the other end. Trying to build that network, trying to get really worthwhile things like pension shares was actually some of the most useful things I've done in my life. But it could only be done in this sort of forum. And it could only be done because we don't have a Speaker, because we do have cross-benchers and because the whip runs fairly lightly. And it all takes place on the floor of the House and therefore the chamber; not the committee room, not the tea room or smoking room, the chamber is the focus of political life here. If you decide to take the House seriously, and you're a fool not too, you could actually do a lot of good things here which you can't possibly do down the other end.

Lady Hollis, Labour

I've been very happy doing what I'm doing now. I think the way my life has worked out outside of politics, it has been much more satisfactory not being in the Commons that I never really gave it a thought - I was so lucky to be able to come here that I haven't thought more about it.

Lord Inglewood, Conservative

I enjoyed being a minister enormously. I enjoyed it back at the time of the great reform of the betting laws (and I'm a keen racing man) a bill very much overdue. It taught me something about politics which is that no matter what your interest is, if you want change in it, it comes down to politics. You'd think horse racing is far away from politics but in the end you get these very necessary changes to legalise off course betting, that can only be done through Parliament. Power is a difficult word. It has all sorts of jackboot connotations. I'd rather put it as the means of getting done what you believe to be right. It has been a useful platform for me. It's a platform, but without a democratic base to your seat you rightly don't have much influence.

My attendance dropped off, I suppose through old age and also I have problems with my eyes so I can't read at all. Therefore if I want to speak I have to memorise the whole thing, which is difficult. Also, I come to London much less than I used to. I'm not quite a backwoodsman, more a middle-woodsman.

Duke of Devonshire, Cross-bencher

I wish I hadn't lost my seat in Battersea. But this gives me a second opportunity to be active in politics on behalf of the Labour Party, with my ability to pursue my own particular interests that I'm committed to, like refugees and asylum. Doors open as they did before, and it's a platform for the same causes that motivated me when I was in the Commons. So it's an opportunity to go on being active in national politics and use parliamentary methods to further that.

Lord Dubs, Labour

What I don't get out of it is either money or an office. But I don't mind because that actually means you meet people. You inevitably meet people: you are not surrounded by a machine. And it's not like the American Senate where you have your own work cut out by having to administer a staff of 40 or 60 or 80. So what I get out of this is a continued, if marginal, participation in the political process. That's the main source of satisfaction and that in an atmosphere which is not overheated.

Lord Dahrendorf, Liberal Democrat

I shall be sorry to see it all go. Personally I've had a wonderful time. I've managed to get to understand things, which before I had not understood very clearly. I've got to meet a lot of very interesting and often very intelligent people. One of the great delights of the House of Lords is that you can find conversation. That you can find in good clubs, of course, and that's what it is. It is a very good club. A club they pay you to attend. I think it's more difficult for women peers, a lot of the baronesses, because women don't have this tradition of clubs here. Men join clubs because they can feel free and easy and behave childishly.

Lord Falkland, Liberal Democrat

I enjoy it. You get interested in a subject. I took quite a big part towards the end of the last Tory Government with the Housing Bill which I got very interested in. You get information notes from outside which of course are a great help. I've also specialised for many years now in the Arts. I have a great many friends now outside. I know most of the people in the art world and you get suggestions for speeches and help and so on, and I enjoy speaking on these subjects.

Lord Strabolgi, Labour

'It's a dotty system, which has me in it's Upper Chamber.' But having said that we have a great privilege, and we owe it to try to give something back for the privilege. It's rather an old-fashioned point of view, but I sincerely believe it to be true. We've had three, three-line whips since I've been a Conservative in the House of Lords. I've disobeyed two of them. I voted for the Referendum on Maastricht; I voted for amendments of the poll tax which I thought was totally iniquitous and a self-evident tax which was going to fail, as I had read a bit of history and know the poll tax has historically always been a disaster. It's undoubtedly fun as well; you get to meet interesting people, you hear things. And the fact that you can meet ministers, and talk to ministers, and it doesn't matter which party - you can go to somebody and you can say "This, this and this happened, can you do something about it, or what should we do?' And I find it equally true with Labour or Tory ministers. Access to power is power itself. Obviously you have to use it extremely rarely, otherwise you'd get a reputation for being a prat.

Earl of Onslow, Conservative

I've got to look at it and say I've been jolly lucky. I've had two things that have been interesting politically, and I hope I made a reasonable fist of it, and that's much more than most people who've been in politics have managed to do. It would be the utmost of people's dreams. So don't be greedy. As a Lords minister I was responsible for a serious and major piece of legislation - the Broadcasting Act. Now, I can look back on my political career and say that's the thing that's got my fingerprints all over it. So, OK the Lords may not be the most important part of the political system but by virtue of being there, I was then involved in doing this work which is affecting everybody in the country. That's something, isn't it?

Lord Inglewood, Conservative

I love It, I thoroughly enjoy it. I meet a lot of very nice people, especially now I've retired. I live and die in the Labour movement and I meet a lot of people in it. You do get the feeling of being in the swim. It's changed now because now we've got government and we shall have to see how far we can influence that government. If we think that government hasn't got it quite right can we improve it? It's a totally different ball game and I just don't know what it's going to be like.

Lord McCarthy, Labour

I don't get kicks about being here in the House of Lords. I get a kick out of being in politics. It's a bonus to me, to be able to retire after 40 years of being a market researcher, and to still have a job to go to which pays decently. It's long hours - a 15 hour a day. Working is always very much fun, and learning things is great fun. I have this wonderful opportunity to do both these things at the age of 64. It's great.

Lord McIntosh, Labour

I love it. It's better than working. I love the place, because it's a continuation. At 65 I became Chief Whip and for seven years I was in full-time, paid employment, pension, all the rest of it. And even if you're not paid, you've still got a modest income from attendance. Whenever you want to take part in politics, you can come to the House, you can debate, put down questions and you continue your life. You don't have to come every day, but you can slacken off, so that anybody who's sent to the House of Lords is very, very lucky.

It is said that to come to the Lords adds five years to a man's life. I don't know whether it's true for women. I wouldn't be at all surprised, although I've not seen the statistics, if that was true, because old men often don't know what to do with themselves. Women don't quite have that problem. But I've discovered, years ago, how difficult the transition to retirement was and how people didn't know what to do with themselves, especially men. Here's one place. For a few.

Lord Dahrendorf, Liberal Democrat

CHAPTER FIVE

Almost a Real Job

IN power terms the Lords do little, in work terms a great deal. Thousands of amendments, nearly all desired by government, are passed and if the Lords fallback didn`t exist, governments would have to invent it. Hundreds of bills are given a final polish or a light dusting. A few, particularly technical and less controversial measures, go first into the Lords arriving, not exactly "to go" in the Commons, but with a lot of the work done; unless as happens on some, such as the 1989 Broadcasting Bill, the Government changes its mind. Again. In all just over half of the time of the Lords is spent on government's legislation, a fifth on general debates and a tenth on questions, with the rest going to debate in committees (3%), delegated legislation (3%), then statements, private members bills and trivia.

This is light legislative work, much of it unskilled. It is very unequally shared out. A minority do most of it, particularly the detail, with most peers putting their hands to the legislative wheel only occasionally. Nevertheless, the Lords do provide hundreds of extra debating, speaking, questioning and intervention opportunities, most usefully on issues which the Commons are less likely to pursue, though this can take the House into the daft and the esoteric. A particular example of this was the issue of the Lord Chancellor's tights, ripped off by a majority of 145 to 115, 80% of the latter were Tories voting for tradition, and two thirds of the former Labour life peers trying to make their hose more comfortable, and Cross-Benchers, unlike tights, evenly split. Sadly, they and the other daftnesses are the only area where The Lords is likely to be reported.

Their work is done with an arcane courtesy which can be more telling than the confrontational Commons which regards clashes as a fun system of government. It is also done by amateurs, which makes it more enjoyable. For the peerforce it's all useful stuff, if minor key. It gives peers a role, an interesting after-life, and a feeling of satisfaction, even though their job has overtones of the circus pensioner mopping up after the elephant and replying to challenges about his come-down in the world by saying, "I'm still in Show Biz aren't I?" So are their Lordships.

The example that always comes to mind is the War Crimes Bill, the first time that the Parliament Act has ever been used. The War Crimes Bill came to the House of Lords having been passed by substantial majorities in the House of Commons, largely as a result of Margaret Thatcher's 'debt' I suppose it was, to the Jews of her own constituency. The Lords rejected it on second reading which really is most unusual because it is traditional in the House of Lords that you give a bill a second reading so that you can examine it, scrutinise it and revise it. On this occasion they were so outraged by the bill that they declined to give it a second reading. It went back to the House of Commons who insisted that they were going to have the Bill. So it came back to the House of Lords where it was rejected for a second time. The Parliament Act had to be implemented. That Act is now not a true Act of Parliament, it's an Act of the House of Commons. I have to say that I took the view on the first occasion of the second reading that I would oppose the Bill, which I did. Then, on the second occasion my view was that the Commons had insisted and I thought that even if the House of Commons wanted to make a fool of itself they must be allowed to do so. So I abstained on that occasion.

Lord Stoddart, Labour

I think the best debates in the House of Lords are absolutely terrific. That's one of the things that would be tragic if the hereditary peers were to be abolished because you'd have a whole lot of really boring politicians, as you do in the House of Commons. I remember one particular debate which I thought was quite exceptional. It was about the war criminals when they were discussing about what should happen and the House of Lords threw it out. It was argued so well in the House of Lords. I knew nothing about it and I just sat there simply riveted by a whole lot of people who were really involved, including quite a lot of Jewish peers as well. I thought it was such a good debate and it was interesting because it was something I hadn't really thought about.

Lord Glasgow, Liberal Democrat

I think it's a very good revising chamber. It could work as a chamber of life peers of course, as it's becoming gradually. It's perhaps two-thirds life peers now, as far as value is concerned. Attendance and value, importance and weight. About a third hereditary. So if it was all life peers I think it could probably continue to work as a revising chamber. Many amendments are sent back to the Commons. Many of the drafting ones are because the government has then conceded different points, but others are where the Lords have made a stand and the government has very often accepted it. I think it would be a great loss, really, if the legislation only went through one House. Many bills, let's face it, come up to the Lords in an imperfect state, and so they are improved considerably. That's one value. The other value is the general debates which are high quality. What is such a pity is that none of this is ever reported. Not much from the Commons is reported and hardly anything from the Lords. The press ignore us. When I first came here, the Times used to give terrific space to parliament in a big debate in the Lords, every peer's speech was reported, even if you were junior people like me who'd only got a couple of lines. There was your name in capital letters and two or three lines given to every single speech. Now, there's absolutely nothing unless something silly is said or there's a cynical repartee in Question Time about smoking in the library or something like that. That gets reported, but nothing serious at all. We have four oral questions a day and Wednesdays are given over to debates, and we have the equilvalent of the closure debate which is an unstarred question which usually takes an hour and a half, or sometimes just an hour, during the dinner hour.

Lord Strabolgi, Labour

The crucial thing here is we don't have a Speaker so the House keeps itself in order. There's a premium on etiquette, courtesies of a fairly flowery nature. Don't be deceived. You say absolutely sharp things. You just say it in this rather different language of the 18th century court. It's finesse rather than sledgehammers. That's fine and the virtue of that means that you don't get the "yah-boo" little boy breadroll throwing style in the Commons, which I think is pitiful. You actually get a much more adult discourse. Women are heard much more easily here because you don't get the heckling, the barracking, the rudeness and interruptions. You get none of that here.

Lady Hollis, Labour

I would prefer to be in the Commons because it is the real theatre of politics. That is where the great game is played and I think that if you have political ambitions you've got to test those ambitions and skills in the real arena, which is the Commons. A number of people who admire the Lords because it is more genteel and the debates more orderly don't appreciate that the conflict of the Commons actually tests the Government. Ministers in the Lords really get a very gentle ride, and it would be intolerable if you had the same gentility in the Commons. It's difficult enough to check and balance the Executive in our system without building good manners into it as well. Some of the things that people see as faults in the Commons are really part of the necessary checks against a very powerful executive that we have in our system.

Lord McNally, Liberal Democrat

It does three things very well. It acts as a house of influence using the weapon of time in the legislative programme for negotiating concessions with the government. As a former business manager in the government I always used to find that come about February or March people would say, "Oops, we're not going to complete the legislative programme" and the logjam, as always, tends to be the House of Lords. So you have to go off to the Opposition and say, with your arm firmly up behind your back, "half a loaf", and if they're sensible they'll say "three quarters" and then you say, "done". That's how the House of Lords really operates as the house of influence. It's a moderating influence. That's especially true in an age were there's far too much ill-digested and ill-prepared legislation a lot of which, particularly in this parliament, is not even considered by the House of Commons. Large chunks of the Scotland and Wales Bill, for instance, haven't been discussed by the House of Commons at all. If you have a House of Lords which is able to make the government answer questions, sometimes they're shamed into realising that the legislation they put forward in such a hurry is not going to work.

They do provide an awful lot of amendments in this House. For instance I think I'm right in saying that in the current session there have been nearly 2000 amendments passed by the House of Lords, a large proportion of them proposed by the government; 98% of them have been accepted by the House of Commons. That is evidence I think of the inadequacy which hurriedly prepared legislation creates.

Lord Cranborne, Conservative

It's always said that our role is as a revising chamber and I think we do provide extra time for government legislation to be scrutinized in considerable detail, very often by people of great knowledge. And I have to say I think there is a lot to be said for the system whereby a lot of those who are here as a result of patronage can take part; for example, the number of Law Lords who've been dealing with the Crime and Disorder Bill. One might not necessarily always agree with what they want to do but that could always be overturned in the Commons - the House which represents the popular will. But at least the arguments have been considered and I think it is probably on that where it performs best.

We do obviously spend quite a lot of other time on debates on all sorts of matters, some which receive some coverage, some which receive none whatsoever, but occasionally they can be quite a useful way of airing views. Not always. Roy Hattersley prefers to use the newspapers - and quite right. He probably reckons that he gets greater coverage.

Lord Henley, Conservative

The Speaker of the House of Commons is in charge of the standing orders while the Speaker of the House of Lords is in charge of nothing except to put the question. The standing orders of the House of Lords, in so far as there are any, are the prerogative of the House of Lords itself, and if there is any disagreement about them they will vote. They will get advice from the Leader of the House but certainly none from the Speaker because he's not allowed to give advice.

I found it extremely strange being in the House of Lords and not having to be called to ask a supplementary question or to make an intervention. People just get up and speak. If somebody from the Opposition gets up and if you think it`s their turn you give way. It works by courtesy. I never thought I would see an organisation like this being able to conduct its own business without certain imposed discipline, but, in fact, it works extremely well.

The other beauty of the House of Lords, and this is why it`s much more democratic than the House of Commons, is that if anybody wishes to speak on a bill, for example, or a debate they are allowed to speak. Nobody calls you to speak. For convenience on a second reading if you wish to speak you put your name down, and the House will go on and on until everybody who wishes to be heard has been heard.

Lord Stoddart, Labour

The Lord Chancellor presides on the Woolsack but he has no power over the discipline of the House. This is quite different to the Commons. If things go wrong in the House, or an individual peer has to be brought to attention, that is the responsibility of the Leader of the House, representing the House as a whole. There is no chair to an extent which is rather frustrating when you're sitting on the Woolsack. Committees are taken on the floor of the House, and if you chair the committee, as I have done, you are just there to put the questions and put the motions. But no more. But we are now beginning to have committees in the Moses Room which is a good idea, not always on the floor of the House. We select bills that are non-party really, like the Lottery Bill , that kind of thing. They work very well, and they take up a good deal of time that would otherwise be spent in the Chamber.

As chairman, first of all you call the amendment, "Lord so and so, amendment 22". Then he makes his speech, and at the end of his speech, you ask, "Is it your Lordship's pleasure that the amendment be withdrawn?" If he resists and says no, he wants to test the feeling of the House, you then have to put the question, "Is this amendment agreed to?" then "Content or not content?" If there's a dissent on both sides you have to clear the bar during division and read out the result at the end.

You can't shut people up. The ones to do that is the Leader of the House. If it's not of a very topical interest, the Leader of the House will then get up and say, "I'm sure it will be the wish of the House that we should now move on to the next question." That is never questioned. If some speech on a policy is too long the House then gets rather restive. We are increasingly having more timed debates now so the bigger debates are timed for five hours, and the times are then worked out. The government spokesman is given 15 or 20 minutes, the initiator of the debate a similar time, then the rest of the time is divided up amongst the rest of the speakers, so you get 10 minutes, 12, sometimes six, sometimes five. You have to keep to that. Otherwise they get rather restive. A peer could get up and say, "The noble Lord has now been on his feet for 15 minutes and he's only allowed 12". When there's a timed debate, at the end of Questions before it starts, the Chief Whip will read out how long peers are allowed. Then he'll say, "I'd like to remind the House that if peers exceed this time, it's at the expense of other speakers." If they do it you don't speak to them in the bar and they get ticked off in the corridors, if they don't play the game.

Lord Strabolgi, Labour

The other thing that is totally different from the Commons is taking bills on the floor of the House, so that everybody is on every committee. Therefore, it is a matter of choice whether you decide to make the Education Bill your particular hobby horse. So you'll get the front benches behaving very much as front benches do in the Commons, but you then find that you may get another half dozen or a dozen people who will self select to work through a bill and come up with amendments.

Amendments are much easier to table in the Lords. A lot of the amendments are put through by lobbyists or interest groups. The lobbyists find that the Lords is a place where they can make an impact directly. If there's a debate and you've shown an interest you will get a sheaf of briefing papers and background notes from various interest and lobby groups to help you with your speech. The Lords is so open that it almost doesn't need the kind of heavy lobbying you get in the commons. If you can get a member interested you can brief him or her and they can take part in the committee and they can table an amendment.

Lord McNally, Liberal Democrat

What the House of Lords does is add to the three stages of scrutiny of legislation, four further stages because we have third reading, as well as report. The changes that we make, other than the changes government wants to make because it hadn't thought of them before, are minimal. We make really very few changes to legislation which would not otherwise have been made or which are not overturned, quite rightly, by the Commons when they go to the Commons. And we give way. The only serious exception I can think of to that, is the Greater London GLC Abilition Bill which would have handed over power from a Labour GLC to a Tory dominated quango. It was an outrage, and the government gave way.

Any other changes in the 15 years that I've been here have been neither important nor adequate to justify the delay that takes place. On all the rest of it, the debates of senior people and distinguished Lords, I have always taken the view that when I look at the allotment holders at Highgate   allotments they would make just as good a second chamber as the House of Lords. The advantage of this place is that there's an awful lot of amateurs as politicians, whose main interest is not in politics. But at the same time, they're the kind of people I've been avoiding all my life. Tall, rich, public school, male. If I wanted that sort of thing, I would have joined a London club.

Lord McIntosh, Labour

One of the jobs of the House of Lords which almost nobody understands is to scrutinise legislation. It`s job is to take a bill and take it apart line by line and look at it and make sure that it actually stacks up. That, in many cases, doesn't actually have to be political. You're questioning how it was drafted, you're questioning the idea behind it.

Lord Redesdale, Liberal Democrat

As a minister you do have to concede on occasion that we haven't got the absolutely perfect answer. That's more respected than it would be in the Commons. More frankness gets elicited from those areas where the Opposition or backbenchers are tenacious. You get brownie points for it and it makes the next thing slightly easier. If you just keep repeating the main line of the slogans or the departmental brief it makes life more difficult. Also I suppose it does improve the quality of debate.

Question Time is more difficult here. You don't have a howling opposition, but we only have four questions a day so it's basically eight minutes per question. So you get roughly seven supplementaries. Foreign affairs have got generals here who fought in these countries or conquered them or handed them over, or people with investments, or deep prejudices, with very humanitarian efforts and concerns. So there are parts of the world here which never get touched on in the House of Commons, and a level of expertise. Some pretty eccentric contributions as well but also deep prejudices about various parts of the world. You don't quite know what's going to come at you, and quite often, even if you've got briefing for 50 supplementaries, it won't quite cover the point that's being raised.

Lord Whitty, Labour

It's not about power, it's actually about getting through the process, taking right decisions to benefit the ultimate customer. My business has always been customer-focused. And you don't use power to achieve that. What you do is, by process of debate, by analysis, you arrive at the right decisions. OK, you have the ability to take those decisions in business, whereas you don't have the ability to take those decisions here. But you've got just as much influence in this place as you do on a board. You really do.

Lady O'Cathain, Conservative

All the constitutional debates about what the House Lords does are complete crap. The House of Lords is not, except on very rare occasions, a revising chamber. It doesn't improve the quality of legislation, it just mimics the committee stages, but on the floor of the House, thereby wasting time.

Defeats for the government in the House of Lords are not because they've improved the legislation, generally speaking. They are because there is a Liberal opposition. So it's not really a revising chamber, nor is it a proper scrutiny on the executive which the constitutional books will say it is. What it is is an attempt to kid itself that it's an equivalent chamber to the House of Commons. It's not, and a reformed chamber will not be.

Lord Whitty, Labour

I think the old Attlee advice is good, "Specialise and stay out of the bars". Certainly the "specialise" part is still worth following. I think you are more listened to if you have established yourself as knowledgeable in a particular area and you do your homework. It's a very interesting House because when the specialist debates take place it does produce a real raft of expertise. The education debates in here - the Vice Chancellors come out of the wood and work like nobody's business - and the defence debates bring out the generals and the military men. They don't dominate the debate but they bring a perspective of professional experience which I don't think you get now in the Commons as the Commons itself becomes more professional politicians rather than "ex" this or "ex" that.

There are many more "exes" with substantial experience in the Lords than is the case with the Commons. When there is a defence debate and two or three former Chiefs of Staff stand up and give warnings it makes government pause. That's as much as it should do. It should make people think and make them justify their policies. In that respect it earns its corn. In my view, that's as much power as a second chamber that doesn't have a democratic mandate, should have. It should be a kind of light rein on government, it shouldn't be able to disrupt and destroy a programme. That's also the case for reform because no matter how responsible the Conservative in-built majority is, there is a temptation - as you get into the second half of the parliament - to use the powers of delay that the Lords have for purely party political ends. That means that non-Conservative governments only get three years rather than five.

Lord McNally, Liberal Democrat

The order of speaking is done by the whips but each individual can make representations and say I would like to be in this position or that position, then they'll consult. I have not yet seen anybody quarrel with their order because I'm quite sure that they look at the number of times a person has spoken and where that order is. But the main fact is that if you want to speak, you will speak and I've known the House go on until the early hours. It is a very democratic place. I was amazed. I didn't think it could work, but it works extremely well. There's a lot of courtesy here, there's a lot of friendship here, and there are people whom I meet and talk to that I never would have dreamed that I would be friendly with in the Commons. So one's view changes. The other point is whilst we don't have Standing Committees we do have Select Committees and one of the most important Select Committees is the Select Committee on European Affairs which has five sub-committees. They not only examine bills in relation to whether they're in order, they look at Regulations and Directives and whatnot. They actually examine the   policy content and they summon witnesses and they produce very good reports.

Lord Stoddart, Labour

Very often it's only when it's been through the Commons that various interest or pressure groups wake up to the fact that they are going to be affected by the legislation that's going through. Then they come along and say, "This is what we'd like to have done to it." This is where most of our amendments derive from. The more professional ones come to us at a very early stage. The sad ones are the ones that wake up too late and write us long arguments after the report stage has gone by. It's no good saying, "This is a terrible bill, get rid of it." We had a lot of that during the guns business. I had more correspondence about that than anything I've ever had. And, whichever side of the argument you were on, it was very sad to find these people writing to you at a point where a) there was nothing more you could do and b) what they really wanted was the Bill to be scrapped. The House of Lords won't do that.

Lord Tordoff, Liberal Democrat

We have some eccentrics here. Pretty ludicrous axe-grinding contributions. Then again, occasionally if we have a debate on defence, you have a few generals putting in a valid viewpoint and then lawyers on constitutional issues. By and large it doesn't ever get quite as trivial as the Commons gets. But quality is not quite the word that I would ascribe to it. I think diversity, and occasionally a bit of good common sense from people who've been practitioners in the area we're discussing, which politicians rarely are. But you couldn't say this was the place you'd come if you really wanted to hear the best of sense. I remember when the Tories were still in power and Michael Howard brought the gun law in, I had some doubts whether this was a sensible piece of legislation. Until I saw the Lords who were opposing it.

You get batty people with concerns about particular parts of the world. I deal with foreign affairs, and the Earl of Carlisle who's a lovely chap, he's lived most of his life in Estonia. He raises Estonia at least once every three weeks and makes fairly wide-ranging speeches. I don't know how long the Earl of Carlisle goes back but it's a long way, and he's ended up by being here as a representative, effectively, of the Estonian government.

Lord Whitty, Labour

It's very rare that the Lords leads the news or is carried in the paper. Our media are very poor at covering Parliament and make no effort to cover it properly. The people who are affected by any particular debate - the Aid lobby, the Foreign Affairs, Defence, whatever - you very quickly find if you make a speech in a particular debate you will get letters from representatives from the interest groups. It is more noticed than you would imagine simply by looking at the cuttings file from the national press.

I get around 30 or 40 letters a week whilst as an MP I'd get probably ten times that amount. As a peer you've got no constituency interests, so the letters are almost entirely from interest groups and a few from the general public. But there's not a constant flow of requests for action, none of the kind of ombudsman-cum-social worker role that an MP increasingly has, and of course there are no constituents. So the mail is probably more specialised.

Lord McNally, Liberal Democrat

In a situation where the government is not threatened, civil servants can hear from the opposition parties what their amendments actually mean, and vice versa; the government can explain rather more easily to opposition parties what their clause in the bill means. A lot of the toing and froing is because people aren't explaining themselves very clearly.

Lord Tordoff, Liberal Democrat

We have the short debates. They are mostly in the Autumn in the early part of the year before the House gets really very busy with legislation coming up from the Commons. And they're for two and a half hours. We have two in an afternoon, two two-and-a-half hour debates, and they are balloted for so they take the ones from the order paper where there are usually 10 or 12. They put them in a hat and in the presence of the three whips they are then drawn out and the first two are put down for that day.

Lord Strabolgi, Labour

We don't have committees here which seriously scrutinize what the executive does, except a little bit in the European Select Committee and the Science and Technology Committee. But they're the only two executive scrutiny committees that we've got. They're very high quality. But they don't have much of the mainstream of political life all the areas of economic and social policy are not really covered by them, unless they happen to have a European dimension.

Lord Whitty, Labour

The select committees in the Lords are quite different to the Commons in the sense that they are horizontal committees, but not departmental committees. You've got science and technology which usually has set committees, and the thing that I'm supposed to be in charge of - the European Communities Select Committee. And they go across departments, on issues or documents or whatever. We never have any difficulty in getting people to come and talk to us. The changes in the Amsterdam Treaty I hope will actually improve our ability to scrutinize European legislation better, because they've now built in this six-week time period.

The system falls down in the Commons because the government really doesn't provide enough time for things to be done properly. Whereas here, we tend to pick out a few selective issues and study them in depth. We've got six sub-committees looking at things according to subject and we will appoint a specialist advisor and take some months over taking evidence both from the department, a minister, people outside, Brussels and so on.

We do have people here with a wide range of expertise in different subjects. Our environment sub-committee has Lord Lewis of Newham who was the president of the Royal Society of Chemistry. So when he says that the water directive from Brussels is based on a very unsound scientific base, he's liable to be listened to. Until recently, we had two Nobel Prize winners on Chemistry in the House, to say nothing of all the legal expertise we have.

Lord Tordoff, Liberal Democrat

Most peers, when they come to this House, soon get into the way of it. You can still give a passionate speech. But the speeches here are not quite as passionate as, perhaps, they are in the Commons. It's a different approach and different technique. Shackleton used to say, "In the House of Lords, oil gets into the veins", and it does.

Lord Strabolgi, Labour

We now sit pretty long hours, I think the second longest number of hours of any legislative body in the world, the longest being the Commons. In government we were here frequently until 11 o'clock because it is up to the government to keep the House, and the government only really has its payroll vote to count on. Often it was the ministers who were expected to stay so for the last eight years, on Mondays, Tuesdays and Thursdays, it was actually quite difficult to make arrangements to go out, dinner, opera or whatever. On top of that, we're in the House more often than our Common's counterparts because - take education - if there's one minister in the Lords, and five in the Commons, by definition I need to be doing four or five times more than they are in terms of parliamentary business.

One of the great joys of opposition is that I'm not tied to the House in the same way. It's now the government who've got to keep the House and persuade their ministers and others to stay behind. We only need to have two or three to take through whatever the business is.

Lord Henley, Conservative

The Labour front bench people are performing very well indeed. Already they're getting their heads out of the briefs, and they've got a command of their briefs and not just reading everything that's on paper. The other thing to notice is that the Conservative ex-ministers are having to write their own speeches. Although I think they're beginning to learn how to do that, the first few weeks were terrible because they were just recyling all their election broadcasts, to the great boredom of everybody.

Lord Tordoff, Liberal Democrat

There are the small things of no longer having the benefits of the civil service behind you, and I do have to say the Private Office system does provide ministers with the most wonderful support that I think very few other people have, in whatever walk of life they're in. You suddenly find you've got to start running your own diary and all that. I think the big change is finding you've got an awful lot more to do yourself, but also, finding there's an awful lot you don't have to do.

If I take legislation going through Parliament at the moment - the Crime and Disorder Bill - I'm leading for the Opposition on that. Now obviously we want to make sure that the government adequately explain what they're doing and argue out their case the whole way through it. That means one's got to put down quite a lot of amendments to make sure you can argue it out. I did

97

find that process of drafting amendments, getting them together, finding other people to draft them for me, quite a difficult job. Once you get into committee stage, it's actually much more relaxing. It's up to the government to explain and I intervene as and when I wish. The government have to concentrate the full eight hours or whatever. In opposition one can have a more relaxed time. Also in opposition, if I dare say, one can be slightly more irresponsible. I remember the remarks of Robin Cook - one should enjoy one's time in opposition, but not enjoy it too much.

Lord Henley, Conservative

It's a kind of traumatic experience to cross the House. Particularly after the defeat of 1st May 1997 which was of a quite different order than the defeat of 1974 had been. I think that the difference is the proposal of the Labour Party to abolish the right of hereditary peers to sit and vote in the House. There is no doubt that this rides like a kind of undercurrent in the House. I think the political complexion has changed too, obviously with the influx of far more Labour life peers, and I understand still more to come. The Labour Party wanted to correct the balance so enormous numbers of new life peers have come. One's got to get to know their names and who they all are, that kind of thing. I think it's become more political. And I've noticed, from time to time, a sort of tetchiness which I haven't really seen before. Nobody I think is rude. That would be very un-House of Lords but I just have a feeling that people on both sides are finding it slightly more stressful.

Lady Young, Conservative

There's much more research available for MPs in opposition than there are for peers in opposition on the front bench. We have a limited amount of research. The advantage we've got is that we've actually got a lot of other people about, who have a very detailed knowledge. That may not be necessarily a very wide knowledge but you probably find someone on your side who really knows the ins and outs. I'm doing Environment, the Regions, and Transport as opposition spokesman. So on those kind of environment things I've got a pretty clear understanding of what the nubs of the issues are. You don't have to have huge detailed knowledge of exactly where the proposed housing development outside Stevenage is, but you know if they're talking about an area inside of a thousand acres of the greenbelt, you understand immediately what the implications of that are. Anyway, a decent lawyer can make a case with the material he's got.

Lord Inglewood, Conservative

Over the last 20 years it has changed by becoming more and more like the House of Commons. And that's a weakness. I'm a great supporter of the House of Commons, and you've got to be able to look after yourself to be listened to. But the House of Lords, that's not their role. Their role is to have a look at what the Commons does. The ultimate power is in the Commons. All that we can do, which I think is done very effectively - and was done even more effectively 20 years ago - is to look at it and point out the weaknesses if there are any, or to give suggestions. If they're better than what the government of the day was wanting to do from the Commons, you send it back.

Lord Harmar-Nicholls, Conservative

Another issue in which I was involved was the Railways Bill. We felt very strongly, like the Labour Party, that it should not be privatised. This included a lot of the Conservatives as well. But the government was determined to put it through and nothing could be done about it. In the end, it was actually the Liberals that said, "We think the government is making a great mistake by privatising the railways, but we are the non-elected House and we've made our point. We therefore, are not going to put it to a vote again and we're not going to stand up to the government". That's very sad. If we're going to have any powers, I think at least we shouldn't be afraid to use those very limited powers. But at the moment we're afraid to use them. Which is rather sad, and it's entirely because we feel embarrassed about ourselves.

Lord Glasgow, Liberal Democrat

CHAPTER SIX

Party Matters

The rise of Government by Party has ensured that the Commons has been transformed and is now run and dominated by the party of government. That process is incomplete in the Lords because they're so much less important. With the rise of mass political parties from the Second (1867) Reform Bill, party took over the Commons subordinating it to what is, in effect, a second chamber role. Today, the real first chamber is the cabinet and the leadership nucleus of the governing party. The Commons, the rumpus room of the constitution, merely ratifies their decisions after testing them in a rowdy confrontation meant to put the argument before the people. In smaller parliaments in more democratic countries like Australia and New Zealand, the caucus of the parliamentary party becomes the real first chamber. It has a democratic influence over a cabinet which must get the consent and support of the party before putting policies and legislation into the House. Not so here where British parliamentary parties are too big to be anything but sounding boards for ministers and climbing frames for the careerist. Majority party MPs are there to vote for the cabinet's decisions not to frustrate or reject them.

This is Government by Party. In this system the Lords are effectively the third rather than the second chamber. The leadership nucleus of the governing party is both the executive and effective (but undemocratic) first chamber consulting with interest and focus groups to formulate policy. The executive runs the Commons, providing its agenda, controlling its business, and pushing its own proposals through. The Commons, effectively a second chamber, are basically a rubber stamp for the executive, and a testing ground in which governmental proposals - and ministers - can be discussed and tested. This is the stage on which the four year election campaign is fought to put party cases before an electorate which hardly seems to be listening. After that the role of

the Lords is to give a final polish. The growth of party control in the
Commons from the 1870s onward, and the need to tighten procedures to
counter Irish disruption in the 1880s, influenced the Lords but never to the
same extent. They were less important, particularly after peer power was
broken by the 1911 Parliament Act which reduced the second chamber to a
necessary but subordinate role. Their job was to polish and hopefully (but not
necessarily) perfect the legislative products of a first chamber that was usually too busy putting the argument to do the detailed work.

So the Lords remained what the Commons once were: a self-disciplining
rather than a party-driven body; more relaxed because the party clash is less
intense; less predictable because members can't be controlled or disciplined.
So the past lives on in an institution where most members belong to a party,
but where the parties are less cohesive, less united are and required to com-
pete for the votes of independent members, the cross-benchers, who decline
any party whip. These are 19th century parties functioning in an 18th century House.

The party political side has become stronger. In my grandfather's day he said
that the really nice thing about it was that it was considered rather bad form
to make a party political point at all.

Lord Cranborne, Conservative

It was easier in the old days, in the '60s. Because we weren't expected to win
in the Commons, they never expected us to win the votes in the Lords. In fact,
they rather liked it if we didn't because it was another nail in the coffin of the
House. But since then, or since the last election, the Prime Minister has
arranged for a great many peers to be created. They're very useful, some of
them. Most of them. So having given us, what, 40 peers or so, we're now
expected to win divisions and if we don't there's a great deal of disappoint-
ment down at the other end. We do win most of them but we don't win all of
them so this must place a great strain on the whips, but we get by.

Lord Strabolgi, Labour

There is a whip but it is actually looser. You find that people do defy the
whip, not on every occasion, but they use their minds in a more independent

way, in my view, and I think that's a very good thing for democracy. I defied it in relation to Michael Howard's Bill, but that was because of my experience in the courts. I didn't see it as defiance. I just saw it as using my own common sense.

I'm not a rebel, per se. I do believe in party loyalty but I think you can't leave your brain at home. I just try to use my brain and listen to the arguments. You're mixing with these people every day and the House of Lords is very sociable. If you get a reputation for being a rebel or an awkward sort of character, there's an indirect pressure.

Lord Taylor, Conservative

The Conservatives oppose, quite deeply and ideologically, a lot of what the Labour Government is bringing in, whereas we in the Labour Party tend to think that we are all consensual. New Labour is talking "community" but the old Tory forces are still here. One thing that does amaze you is the number of things that the Tory lords do. To some extent the cross-benchers, and even some of ours, are on so many committees that actually run middle England, or alternative England. They may not be vast powers. They can't confront multinational companies. But they actually run the style of life in a lot of parts of the world. Hunting is a symbol of the end of that. It represents a whole way of life which they feel that even the New Labour Government, which is trying to be consensual, is seriously threatening. It comes out from time to time in education. It comes out on some of the devolution issues, and it will certainly come out on the whole question of reform of the House of Lords which they will regard as far more important in protecting their own self-interests.

Lord Whitty, Labour

I take the Conservative whip, but I've never felt duty-bound, just because I'm there, to do what Mr Heath, Mr Major, Mrs Thatcher, or in future, Mr Hague tell me to. I'm there on my honour, and that's the only way one can see it. On the whole I am a Conservative, whatever that may mean now. I never vote against the government, unless I've listened to the rubbish they're talking. If I think I'm going to vote against them, I go and listen. I listen to the arguments put forward and on occasions I've thought "this is a very bad idea", and I have been converted. Ditto the other way round. I've gone in thinking this is quite a good idea and the most appalling drudge turned up, and I voted the other way. I've done that when both parties have been in power.

Earl of Onslow, Conservative

We can attend PLP meetings, which I try to do. We can be members of the Labour Party backbench groups. We can be members of all party groups so through that structure, we can mix with the Commons. I like to do that because I like to get the sense of what's going on in the Commons, what the issues are and the politics of it. Within the Lords we also have a weekly meeting of Labour peers on a Thursday, and we discuss the business, get reports of the shadow cabinet meetings, reports of PLP meetings and we discuss the week's business. We occasionally have a speaker, often some front bencher from the Commons.

The total number of Labour peers is about 100, if you allow for the people who are ill or too old to make it unless there's a desperate need for their vote and then you have to cajole them. If we get 70 to 80 votes in that's pretty good but I suppose on average at such a meeting we might get between 40 and 60, depending on the occasion. It's not a bad turnout. It's at about two o'clock every Thursday. The whips meet at one and the front bench meet at one thirty, and the party meets at two.

Lord Dubs, Labour

I do enjoy the job but on my own terms. I won't toe any rigid line which is against the things that I believe in. That makes me an awkward cuss. I go to party meetings. I always like to hear what the other side are thinking. Most of them affect to think that I'm obsolete because they are most anxious not to appear out of the running themselves, for future preferment, by getting the reputation that they agree with me. So life can be quite humorous.

Lord Bruce, Labour

We have a party meeting every Thursday and we could also go to the PLP meetings, though we were not allowed to vote. We could speak but not vote. I used to go to the party meetings very regularly but one or two people from the SDP came back and they were welcomed back with acclaim. So I decided I didn't really want any more to do with this lot. I haven't attended meetings since Jack Diamond came back. The meetings are well attended though. In my past experience, proportionally I would say that the House of Lords attendance at party meetings is better than the House of Commons. There now about 125 Labour peers and you would be getting, on average, 45 to 50 attending, and sometimes a lot more. That's a bigger proportion than attend party meetings in the House of Commons.

Lord Stoddart, Labour

In 1979 the Leader of the House chaired the meeting of Labour peers. Ivor Richard, when he became leader of the House, took the view that he didn't wish to be chairman of the Backbench meeting. So the Labour peers accepted his advice that there ought to be one of their number as the chairman. Ivor recommended me to the meeting and they accepted that. We haven't got any standing orders. We're devising them, relying heavily on the PLP. Then I recommended a few colleagues to act as a coordinating committee. They guide me - but after October, they'll be elected. The Labour peers have their own meeting and government ministers in the Lords regularly report to their colleagues and explain the legislation. They defend criticisms offered etc. They're a lively bunch when it comes to their own business.

Lord Graham, Labour

The Association of Conservative Peers meets once a week and has special meetings from time to time. It's a big and rather diffuse group. We're amateurs in the sense that we're part-time, we're sort of semi-professionals in a football analogy. And it's very difficult to guarantee you can be in a particular place at a particular time. It's not only speaking, it's also meetings about one thing and another.

Lord Inglewood, Conservative

There's a Conservative Peers Association with a meeting every Thursday at 2.30. It's a very good turnout. You often have a shadow minister speaking. In power it might be a minister from the Commons. Usually you can get about 100 Certainly the one after the election was, I'd say a 150. The room was packed. But it's a good turnout and we discuss policy and the way forward. We can't help to choose the leader. What we can do is express a view and know that our views put on paper are reflected through to the other MPs, but whether they take any notice, I don't know.

Lord Taylor, Conservative

We meet on Thursdays, from two to three. The Lords starts at 3 o'clock rather than at 2.30 on Thursdays, and all parties meet usually at 2.30. Ours is attended by 30 to 40 people each week, so it's a well-attended meeting. We go through the business of the next ten days. The purpose of the extra half-hour is precisely to talk about some major issue, either a bill coming up, or our general line on it. Or we have one of the parliamentary spokesmen in, or we have Paddy in to talk about some other issue. That's actually quite useful. Up until the election, with a small party in the Commons, there was supposed to be liaison between spokesmen in the Lords and in the Commons, but I got very to turning up in the Commons lobby to meet Charles Kennedy to get a message that unfortunately he was in Inverness or whatever it was. Since the election, partly because we have a larger Commons party, there are weekly team meetings on most issues.

Lord Wallace, Liberal Democrat

The advantage we've got here over our colleages in the Commons is that we Liberal Democrats have always been recognized as the third party. We have always had the right to make the third speech in a debate and the next but one to the end of the debate. And anybody here can put their name down to speak at any time. Similarly with amendments. There's no picking of amendments here. Any that goes down can be spoken to. At the committee stage, you can speak as often as you like, though if you want to get anything done you need to go down before 7 o'clock.

Lord Tordoff, Liberal Democrat

The three political parties plus the cross-benchers, meet every Thursday at about 2.30pm, and our Chief Whip goes through the business for the following week. One of the things about it is that they can usually look ahead two or three weeks in the Lords. I think there are about 58 registered Liberal Democrats in the Lords, about 40 active, and we meet, go through the business and assign lead speakers. Anybody else who looks like taking an interest will flag up their interest and say they'll be speaking in the debate as well. There'll be a brief discussion on the likely line to take and discussion of when and where we're going to vote. The Chief Whip will report on whether he's in discussion with his Labour colleague or with the cross-benchers.

We have a small but very efficient whip's office with the redoubtable Celia Thomas running things. It is a very efficiently run little unit and in the closing stages of the Parliament the Liberal Democrats have been regularly polling 35-40 votes in divisions, and being the difference in defeating the government. In that way there is really a feeling that you are actually doing things. I often say I was in the Commons for four years and never defeated the government once, and I was in the House of Lords one month and I think we defeated the government twice. Minor defeats but it's amazing how, as part of the overall picture of a government in decay, it's defeats in the Lords that have had an impact.

Lord McNally, Liberal Democrat

We changed how we function quite radically because we've just changed leader. We had a contested leadership election and I was one of the candidates. One of the reasons wasn that there was a lot of discontent behind the scenes, with the rather lordly way, if you'll excuse the pun, Roy ran the Lords. It was very much d'haut en bas and the combination of Roy and John Harris was felt by some of the younger Lords to be much too old style. We didn't have proper open debates.

What the election campaign gave was an opportunity for a lot of people to say how they thought we should operate, what we should do. That was six months ago. Since then we've doubled the length of our weekly meetings. We have serious discussions about how we should approach various issues and whether we're happy with the line that's coming from the Commons. We are turning out in strength. We have 66, 67 or 68 as our total strength. On a three-line whip, we manage to vote, 40 to 45, which, in Lords terms, is quite astonishingly high. I'm not sure how long we can keep up that sort of pace. But at the moment I think we are working remarkably well.

Lord Wallace, Liberal Democrat

Some 20 odd years ago it was thought there should be some kind of organisation for the cross-benchers and Lady Hilton Foster became the convenor. It was a very loose organisation and she ran it very informally. I think it was generally felt, as we grew in numbers, that we should have a greater say through the usual channels.

I don't think that the two political parties took much notice of cross-benchers. In fact, we were rather resented by them. When I arrived here Lord Carrington actually said to me, "Are you a Whig or a Tory?" That was the view they took of us. When I came to help Lady Hilton Foster she decided to stand down after 21 years and I was elected to this position as convenor. We now have a formal electoral system. I am the only officer. We don't get any Short money and the convenor is not paid, nor should be, and we don't get any staff, like all the other parties, even the Liberals who are much fewer than us. We outnumber them by seven to one.

We are absolutely collegiate. Lord Allen of Abbeydale is a former Home Office minister and a great strength to us. Lord Allenby and I are cavalry officers so we're dash and abandon chaps, and a former Permanent Secretary, assures we don't do anything silly. I have to tell you, it's great fun. We don't have any policy. We're not a party. We don't know how we're going to vote.

We meet on a Thursday. They haven't got to come but between 40 and 50 probably will turn up, not always the same people. We don't issue a whip but we send a report out on all our notice boards of what has happened. We issue a forthcoming business to tell them exactly what is happening. If anybody is making a maiden speech we offer them an opportunity, if they wish, to come and talk about it with us. I won't mention the name of the peer who came in here yesterday with his maiden speech which was so awful that we had to tell him that it wasn't really appropriate for this subject, that is what we said. Would he go away and think again. He's been back this morning.

Lord Weatherill, Cross-bencher

I think cross-benchers are marginally to the right rather than the left. They've grown in number and they have become genuinely independent. When I was first a member of the House you were mostly sat on the cross-benches because you had held office of profit, such as a civil servant or ex-army or ex-navy, or something like that. One usually knew with all of those when a particular thing came up which way they would vote. Sometimes I was rather surprised to see a particular cross-bencher vote a particular way. But now the cross-benchers react in the way public opinion in the country at large reacts and suddenly they go in a particular way, like some sort of mass crowd movement. Which makes life difficult.

Lord Denham, Conservative

We don't recruit them. They voluntarily join us. Lord Swansea, for instance, has joined us. "I write to inform you that I've made up my mind to resign the Conservative Whip and sit henceforth at the cross-benches. I am taking this action to protest against the action of the government over the Firearms Amendment Bill. This to me is a shameful Bill etc." And he says, "As you are probably aware I am an infrequent speaker, speaking only on those subjects on which I have knowledge. Nevertheless, I am sure I shall find company congenial on your benches and I look forward to making your acquaintance".

Lord Weatherill, Cross-bencher

There are about 300 cross-benchers of which I think over 60% are hereditaries. They really are the guardians of the ethos of the House now. Quite a lot of the backbenches of various parties are as well but I think they'd find it more difficult if the cross-benchers weren't so strong. It's a pretty powerful combination as it is within the House itself because it's this extraordinary mixture of snaggle-toothed Earls and Nobel Prize winners and former civil servants. They say they don't have a cross-bench view. That's not my experience. They also have something else which I think is important. The only reason this House works at all is because we proceed by agreement. There is an underlying rule which we all abide by which is that the Queen's government must be carried on. The government must get its business through. That's true of the House of Commons but it's true in spades here. The outward and visible sign of that is that on the whole cross-benchers tend to divide when they vote: two thirds, one third in favour of the government no matter what the government of the day is. I think that is quite important. Underpinning that is that Thomas, Tory Chief Whip, and his opposite number through the usual channels do agree on what the future business of the House will be. If there is a disagreement it's universally seen as a failure. The whole thing will break down.

Lord Cranborne, Conservative

It's traditional for whips never to allow people to listen to the arguments. The Leader of the House gave me a drink just before Christmas 1996 and said, "It is our perception since you became the convenor that we seem to be defeated rather more than we used to be in the past. Are you issuing a whip?" "Certainly not" I said. He said, "Well, what's happened then?" I said, "Well, I merely invite them to go in the chamber and listen to the argument." "Oh my God, you don't". It's what Parliament is about.

Lord Weatherill, Cross-bencher

I think quite a good measure of what you're doing is if the cross-benchers on the whole are with you. As a rule of thumb in this House, if the cross-benchers are all against you, as a government or as a minister, you do need to think hard and long about what you're doing - whether it really is right. I think it does act as a check and no one can be quite sure how the cross-benchers will react. Certainly in my experience, ministers can't be sure. They may know one or two, but they can't be sure of that. Government whips and Opposition ones can have no idea how they're going to vote.

Lady Young, Conservative

Three times a year we get what in the old Parliament we called a supply day, and the choice of a debate. Tomorrow, for instance, it's Lord Carnarvon's, one of our number. He's moving a motion on the governance of London, the future of London, the Mayor for London, and over 26 speakers put in. Two maiden speakers from the cross-benches, the new Lord Tweedsmuir, who inherited because his brother had no heirs, and Lord Hankey. Both made their maiden speeches. The subject is decided at our Thursday meetings. We discuss what subjects we would like to put down. Lord Chalfont moved a motion on the media and we've had a motion down on the importance of the family. To be quite honest, the thing that always pleases me is that although Parliament and particularly the House of Lords is very seldom reported in the press, we got a very good press and leading articles on our debate. So our debates cover subjects which the political parties wouldn't normally touch but which ought to be discussed in Parliament.

Lord Weatherill, Cross-bencher

I decided to join the cross-benchers, because I want to be independent and I didn't want to be subject to a whip. If you are, you're obliged to vote when the whip is on. I like to listen to the argument. About three years ago, I was sent for by a committee which was putting forward a paper on the future of the House of Lords. They seemed quite surprised that I thought that before you voted in a division, you should actually consider both sides of the argument. That was quite logical to me, but it didn't appear to be to the others. But I actually think that's the beauty of being a cross-bencher.

Lady Wharton, Cross-bencher

I did start as a cross-bencher but Lord Shackleton once turned pointedly in my direction to say that some of us were so far to the right that we sit on the cross-benches because we can't think of where else to be. I felt a bit lonely on the cross-benches and felt it would be better to have involvement in the Conservative Party.

Lord Sudeley, Conservative

The cross-benchers in the chamber aren't the force they are on paper because they very properly don't usually vote unless they've listened to the debate. So you don't normally get more than 20 cross-benchers voting, and sometimes a lot less. A record, I think, was on asylum seekers' benefits, where 40 cross-benchers voted, and they carried the majority. They divided 38-2. In the last parliament, there was a standard recipe for winning a division. Two opposition parties, both with their tails up. 80% of the cross-benchers and six or seven government rebels. But to carry 80% of the cross-benchers you really needed a good case. In this parliament, defeating the government is so easy, it's unsporting.

Lord Russell, Liberal Democrat

We don't count the Law Lords and, of course, the bishops . Although we do shove up all our notices in the Law Lords` rooms and in the bishops` rooms. We invite them twice a year when we have a party, the summer party and the Christmas party which is Lady Hilton Foster`s. When I went to see the Law Lords about that they said, "Oh, well we`ll rise early and we can come"

Lord Weatherill, Cross-bencher

For the bishops it works on two sort of levels. First of all we're on duty either two weeks of the year if we're senior or three, if we're fairly junior, when we're required to say prayers. Each day of the year is covered by a bishop saying prayers and the House can't really operate until the prayers have been said. When I'm on duty I write the four days of that week out of my diary and try and put things in - if I'm seeing somebody at 11 o'clock, I'm entertaining somebody at tea again to try to look after the diocese and some of my clergy. It's a great treat for some of the clergy or my colleagues to come and have lunch in the Lords or be a part of it.

I try and use the week constructively and when I'm on duty I work in the library in the morning or see people, and then I reckon to be in the chamber. The convention is really that you don't only take prayers but you act as a kind of chaplain to the House while you're on duty. So that's one level.

Each of us have identified certain interests. My interests are penal affairs, housing and agriculture for obvious reasons being from a rural diocese. The penal affairs thing has been very high profile particularly over the last few years. One tries to contribute to that and that highlights the three difficulties. The first is that is difficult to keep track of legislation unless you're following it on a day to day basis. It's difficult to know what stage any particular bill has reached and where you may usefully make a contribution. The second thing is that the parliamentary timetable bears no resemblance to yours. I've got days in my diary for next year now. If I've wanted to go and do a licensing of a parish they wouldn't take kindly if I said sorry friends, I'm in the House of Lords. The third problem is then actually organising yourself to contribute and collecting the material. Here Lambeth play a good part together with Church House. We get a weekly running sheet of an order of business which Andrew Purkis, the Archbishop's public affairs man, marks off for us.

We also get very well served by the Church House lot, particularly the Board for Social Responsibility. They will help us a great deal. We've begun to work more effectively. We got together a group of us who were particularly interested and committed to the Family Law Bill under the Chairmanship of the Bishop of Liverpool, David Shepherd, and the Bishop of Oxford. We decided that we would try to make a contribution and the Secretary of the Board of Social Responsibility at Church House fed us a lot of the parliamentary briefing. On a particular piece of legislation we get someone to marshall the activity and see it through. We found that's an effective way of working and genuinely we help each other. I've written odd bits for the Bishop of Southwark. We try and work it between us as we all know each other very well and we all get on very well together. Lambeth's helpful, Church House is helpful, and that's how we work it. We're weaving and ducking all the time in a way .

Bishop of Lincoln

The Chief Whip has a lovely office on the West front. Previous to 1979 the Labour Party administered Labour peers through a member of staff in the Commons, but during the early '80s, with Cledwyn Hughes, a great leader, and Tom Ponsonby, a great Labour Chief Whip, they needed someone physically up here. So they got the first one, Lady Shirley Shepherd, another great lady, as the voice and the administrator. Then in time we got two. We managed to get money out of the Short Money - that then provided money for one researcher. The front bench of the government in the '80s had the whole of Whitehall to administer it. We had one researcher to provide the backup. Then we got three researchers after the '87 election. One of the untold stories is that the Labour peers in opposition relied almost completely on pressure groups providing briefs. In the Commons, it might just be another piece of bumpf. In the House of Lords, for the backbenchers, the brief from Shelter, from the Consumers' Association, from the Retail Consortium, was all that they got. Plus the backing from the researchers, who are primarily there to serve the front bench. When you realise that on our bench there were 30 people, one researcher was ridiculous. Now, it's just been changed. We've now got what's called Cranborne money. He got the Treasury to agree that £100,000 should be made payable to the Opposition party. And to the second Opposition party, the Liberals, £30,000. So they've now got far more money than I ever got through the Short Money. But at least the Opposition is better provided for than it was in my time.

Lord Graham, Labour

I first became a whip in '61. So I did three years in government and then there was the 64-70 Labour Government, then there was 70-74 Tory, 74-79 Labour. As a whip in the government you're trying to stop your side being beaten more than the bare minimum of times. Sometimes in opposition you're trying to prevent your people defeating the government too many times. It's rather like driving a car. A dog or chicken runs across the road and if you say to yourself, "I must put my foot on the accelorator", by that time, you've run over it. You put your foot on the brake first, and ask questions afterwards. Very often there's something going wrong in the House and as a whip you get into the habit of being able to stop it. You know instinctively this is what you must do. Sometimes you don't know why you've done it. Until afterwards.

Lord Denham, Conservative

We don't have patronage really. There are trips. Every now and again I would be asked if I had someone to recommend for a quango, where they needed a Scotsman or a Welshman, and you would consult with your leader and you'd put forward but patronage is virtually non-existent up here. Looking across at the other side of the Chamber, at the then government, a host of the quango appointments were made to the Conservatives. One of these days someone should do a real job for the Labour Party by publishing the existing members of the Conservative group in the House of Lords, who either have been or are members of all sorts of bodies.

Lord Graham, Labour

After the miner's election (1974) Labour got in without a majority at all. The Government was thought to last only about three weeks. I took quite a plunge when I accepted to join it. I was appointed deputy Chief Whip and captain of the Yeoman of the Guard which goes with that job. That entailed making a uniform and some people in the Palace thought it wasn't worth making a uniform and suggested that I should wear a morning coat for official duties. The Queen said, 'no', I was to have a uniform. Her Majesty prescribed right and I wore that uniform for five years.

Whipping is different in this House. You have to appeal much more to people's sense of loyalty. You can't bring any pressure to bear. You can't do anything through the constituency party. They know they're here for life. So you have to appeal to their sense of loyalty in order to get results.

Lord Strabolgi, Labour

We've got approximately 120 on the books. Approximately 12 of them are hereditary. People like Frank Longford, and there's nobody like Frank Longford. He's a marvellous man. You've got people like Ponsonby and Nick Rea, and other people. There are 108. I'd discount a dozen of those who never come because they're too ill. The actual live list of Labour peers, hereditary and others, is about 90. Even if you count life peers we've got about 110, the Conservative have got 150. So the percentage of Labour life peers who attend is greater than the Conservatives.

Ivor and I drill into the new people, "You've come up here to work." By and large, they accept. Heseltine brought in the privatisation of the mines. In the Commons, we screamed blue murder but we got nowhere. In the House of Lords there was a great censure battle here which we won. We beat the government on a vote of censure. The previous year, with dissolution, birthday honours, and working peers, the Tories sent up 19 new Tory peers, including Lynda Chalker and John Wakeham, etc. We had nine. Of our nine, eight of them voted. Of their 19, one of them voted. Thatcher, Reece, John Moore; they didn't take their job seriously. Our people are more serious about doing their jobs in the Lords than the Tories are.

Lord Graham, Labour

I've taken the Liberal Democrat whip because like others before me, like Keynes, like Beveridge, I feel without a party whip it's a bit lonely in a political institution and I would like to have a sense of the politics of it. But of course the whips have very few sanctions, or rather the only sanction is shame. But shame is rather an effective instrument in the House of Lords, and so one does think twice before one defies the whips. On the other hand, we all do it every now and again. Shame is often more effective if you are a member of a club in which there is an assumption of common membership. Then you don't particularly want others to feel that you've been a bad man.

Lord Dahrendorf, Liberal Democrat

The thing about the whip in this House is that it is not the job of the whip or even the Chief Whip, to make sure his people vote the right way. Everybody has much more freedom. There was a big Conservative majority, in theory. However there wasn't an overall majority. If you take into account the cross-benchers and the Liberals and the official Opposition, or should I say the then official Opposition which was Labour, the Conservative's didn't have an overall majority. If the other two parties and the cross-benchers all voted against us, we must lose. There were always a number of Conservative rebels at any time because they felt that way. That was a very healthy sign and it was not my job as a whip to go and complain bitterly when people voted against us. I'd complain bitterly if they weren't there. But that's all.

Lord Denham, Conservative

Party discipline in this place is much looser than the other end of the building. Being a Chief Whip is really a very peculiar job. You've got to do it by cajolery all the time. The number of three-line whips that come up here are really pretty small. And you've got to recognize that the Tories have a huge in-built majority here. They've got half the Lloyd George hereditary peers as well on their side. Indeed they've got a number of peerages that were Attlee peerages, like Attlee himself. A whole string of them.

The point about this place is that because you can't de-select people the whips don't have the amount of leverage. It leads to a degree of independence that you don't have in the Commons. A lot of things stem from that. If you want to persuade people, you should speak briefly, and preferably to the point. Most people do because occasionally you can change people's minds, and bills can be changed here in a way they probably can't in the Commons.

One starts from the assumption that the government's probably going to get its bill, particularly any manifesto bill. There may be attempts to do a bit of sabotage on the way. Well, the hereditary peer thing is something where we're in totally unchartered water. But even there, I think the government will get its bill eventually. They may have to invoke the Parliament Act. It wouldn't surprise me. But that's easy enough.

Lord Tordoff, Liberal Democrat

A whip here is very different than in the House of Commons. First, the whips do other things. They act as spokesmen for departments and so one is not sealed silent as they are in the Commons. Secondly, one doesn't actually have the power and the patronage and certainly for most of my time as a minister the Chief Whip always made it clear that what he could do as Chief whip was to get people in. Thereafter, it was up to the minister to argue the case and make sure they voted in the right way, and there are occasions when it is a question of how well the minister does his job.

You can send out a whip, one-line, two-line, three-line. It's very rare that one can use a three-line whip. I can't speak from experience - I never was Chief Whip, just a junior whip, but all one can do is persuade and hope they will respond. I would reckon that the other two parties are much more disciplined and certainly when we were in government one noticed far fewer rebellions on the Labour benches and the Liberal benches, than we experienced on the Conservative benches.

Lord Henley, Conservative

I only normally had one three-line whip in a year, I put the three-line whip in on occasions where it wouldn't embarrass too many of my people. I could always win one division a year, and it's my choice, nobody else's. It's my job to get the government business through as unamended as possible, so it was my choice which I did it on, and the Poll Tax vote was actually one. Tufton Beamish put in an amendment which virtually said, take away clause one, insert a new clause one which cracked the whole of the Poll Tax. It imposed on the government the duty to think up some new way of taxing the local authorities. If that had been carried the whole of the rest of the Bill would have fallen. They would only have had two options: one is to have dropped the bill totally, in other words, the Lords killing a bill; or, to take it back and get it under the Parliament Act, which again would have been the Lords would not have had the time to go through the rest of the bits and pieces of the bill.

So it was totally counter to the Salisbury agreement. That is why people came in in their numbers. Not because there was a particularly strong will. So I put on the strongest whip I could. Instead of saying, your Lordship's attendance is most urgently requested, I put down your Lordship's attendance is required. That brought them in. I didn't have to do anything else. Because it was such an important occasion, because it was an amendment that the House should not have been asked to pass, people did come in in their hundreds to vote against it.

Lord Denham, Conservative

The Chief Whip in government really only has in his absolute control the 22 or 23 on the payroll vote. We don't have these convenient votes at 7 o'clock and 10 o'clock, so it's very important that he has most of his boys and girls here. When we divide, we only have six minutes to get here. That meant that certainly for some of the departments I was in, it was actually quite difficult of an afternoon to stay in the department and make it even with the ministerial car, because of the business of Whitehall and all that. Very often I found that if there was a whip on some legislation I would have to spend the afternoon here.

Lord Henley, Conservative

The newly appointed life peers are having a very difficult time. On Labour's side you're expected to come because we want the votes but speeches, except on debate days, hold up the agenda. They are not going to get jobs, and have got perfectly good jobs outside that they want to keep earning money at. Yet they're required to be here for a vote. They have all the disadvantages of being a backbench MP in the Commons and none of the advantages. They don't have constituency work to justify them. They don't have a salary to justify them. They don't have committee work to jusitify them. On the floor of the House, everybody takes a part and you don't build up an expertise, and there's no pay for it. On long sittings, because we have committee stage and report stage and third reading all taking members on the floor of the House ,we have to have a running whip every day on government business. So from 3 o'clock until the House goes down there's effectively a running whip. Every day. Not votes at 7, votes at 10, votes at 4.30, votes at 6.00, votes at 7.30, maybe an ambush late at night, Every day. If you're a Londoner you could probably weave it in, say leave work in the morning or possibly, if you're a backbencher that is, or some academic teacher or something like that. But if you live outside London, you can't.

Lady Hollis, Labour

I now realise that the whole initiative passes to the Opposition. In the past we took the initiative, we knew what days we were going to divide the House. We knew when the whips were going in, we knew when the votes were going, we knew when the vote was coming in at half past four or half past six. Our people decided that and you knew where you were.

You've no bloody idea where you are now. They might divide the House this afternoon on something. Now it's totally different because we're not making the bullets. So we have sit around waiting for them to fire and we have to have a lot of people up a lot of the time, and a lot of the time when a lot of people are up they never have any divisions because it's up to them. This can't go on. If the Opposition doesn't take the Lords on, the reality of their threat will fade away.

Lord McCarthy, Labour

CHAPTER SEVEN

Protector of the People?

LONG seen as a sleepy backwater, the House of Lords has reinvented itself as defender of the people and changed its image from chamber of privilege to house of independent judgement. It has done both more successfully than any other part of the constitution and done so without benefit of hired help such as PR consultancies, packagers or spin doctors. It seized the opportunity provided by the timid reluctance of the Commons to install television by quickly doing so in 1985 - when the lower House refused - thereby improving its image, raising its profile, and reaching the nation through a coverage which the public quite liked, however little they saw of it. It seized the opportunity of Europe to set up a review committee whose work is not only highly praised but far better than anything the Commons does.

Where the Commons excludes, and obsesively protects its rituals and members, the Lords has opened up, particularly to film and the media: the lords were first televised experimentally in the 60s and, in 1970, they gave documentary cameras (directed by the eldest son of an Earl) full access, following up by establishing their own information unit, going onto the Internet, and beginning to promote themselves and their work. More importantly, they touched a popular chord when they began to defeat the all-powerful Tory Government in the 1980s. Here was the only part of the constitution which could say "No" to Mrs. Thatcher. As they did so the lords became more popular, particularly as she moved on to the wilder shores of ideology, and the feeling built up that the Tories had been there too long.

The defeats were not numerous. Nearly all were reversed in the Commons where the Conservatives had an overwhelming majority almost up to the end. They came at half the rate inflicted on the Labour Government in the 70s

119

which had no majority at all. For Labour the Lords had been a real diffculty, for the Tories it was an inconvenience - sleeping policemen - not a road barrier. But it was the only one. Firing darts at her self-appointed majesty enlivened politics and gave hope so it was popular though perhaps overrated. But it certainly looked more effective than the Labour Opposition plotting for much of the period to abolish them.

The election in 1997 of a new Labour Government in its first and fullest ever flush of popularity with 43% of the vote, brought it face to face with the Lords in which two thirds of the party affiliated peers are Tory, changing the Lords from public protector to Labour problem. Labour has an overwhelming mandate, it drives a steamroller through the Commons. Yet it has no majority in the Lords, where it has been defeated more frequently than its predecessors. Most of these defeats are due to the Tory majority among the hereditary peers, over half of whom take the Tory whip, compared to just over a third of "lifers". If Labour mustered its every peer the Tories could still defeat them with only a third of theirs. The same pattern of partisanship had existed under the Tories. Analysis of votes in the 1988-9 showed 172 Tory Government victories on matters they were promoting and 12 defeats. If the hereditaries are excluded this figure would have been 21 victories, 159 defeats and four draws. Mobilisation of hereditary power against the Tories was welcome, but its use against Labour was very different. It was, as the Sun might have said, 'The Hereditaries Wot Done It'. Wot they had in fact done was to inflict 39 defeats on the Blair Government in Labour`s first long session - a quarter of the divisions which took place compared to between a tenth and a sixth of divisions under the Tories. However some of this occurred because Labour was not mobilising its own members to the full, for the maximum Toty vote was usually 140. Thus the most striking feature of the Lords is not the built-in Tory majority but the ducking, weaving, dodging, absenteeism and manoeuvring which goes on around it to subvert, solidify or sink it. Here is where the action, the cunning and the nous all lie.

---

18 years of Conservative rule has seen the Lords at its best in a way because Conservative people have been very independent-minded and defeated the government on many occasions. I think it's worked very well with the Conservatives in power. But with Labour in power it becomes, on paper, impossible. Even if you took only life peers, you get a Conservative

majority. If you took all the hereditaries, you have another 450 peers and a big Conservative majority. A lot would be independent, Liberal, but it would make a nonsense of it bringing in life peers to make up the numbers.

Lord Longford, Labour

I think the reason why people like myself, Ted Graham, Joe Dean and Jock Stallard were sent here was because we were former whips, and Michael Foot had the foresight to see that Thatcher, with a large majority in'83, was going to ride roughshod over Parliament. He foresaw that what he needed was not the 'great and the good' but the workers, people who had administrative experience and experience of whipping. That's what happened and we made a lot of difference.

We upset people because we were much tougher. We said that the nice gentlemanly arrangements that had previously been made would have to be challenged to some degree. We said we were going to vote on things that perhaps we would never have voted on before. We were going to take a tougher line and make the place a little more political than it had been, and to defeat the government on important political matters. We achieved a lot of government defeats.

One of the amazing things about the House of Lords is that it cares more about democracy than the House of Commons. The unrepresentative House is much better with the constitution and democracy than the elected one is. The House of Commons had passed the GLC paving Bill which wound up the GLC before its proper term of office had expired, and the House of Lords was saying, Oh no you don't. That is quite unacceptable. The people have elect-ed the GLC and it must be allowed to run until its mandate runs out". I would have thought that was what the House of Commons should have done, but it was done by the House of Lords. I remember Ken Livingstone saying to me, "Perhaps we should abolish the House of Commons and not the House of Lords". Whether he'll remember that I don't know.

Lord Stoddart, Labour

One of the first major defeats that Mrs Thatcher had in the House which she felt particularly strongly about, because she had been Minister of Education, was the School Transport vote. I told my opposite numbers down in the House of Commons, I think about eight months before the Bill came to us, that this was going to lose and my opposite number in the House of Commons said, "Don't". I said, "Look, I'm not asking whether it may lose, I'm telling you I'm going to lose it". If I had put a three-line whip on that, I might have lost it and that would have been a disaster, because the magic would have gone out of the three-line whip. The thing about that was that for generations local authorities had been closing down the village schools and for generations the local authorities said, don't worry, we'll always have free transport for your children. This was a Tory government being seen as giving local authorities the opportunity to stop it. Occasionally, we had petitions though not as often as your House. On that occasion, whole villages, the whole bloody lot, number one High Street, number two High Street, number three High Street, wrote their names in and sent in. There was no way we could have won.

Lord Denham, Conservative

It was interesting towards the end of the last parliament that you could feel that the government were having greater difficulty in getting their troops here when it mattered. They'd just stay away. They just felt in their bones that it had gone on too long.

Lord Tordoff, Liberal Democrat

If you haven't got backwoodsmen in listening to you, then that's your failure to work the tea room and the library. I'm serious about wanting to get the backwoodsmen either abstaining or voting with me. It's my job to make sure they know about it and that means being here, going to tea, going to the library, talking to them, asking them to come in. In the Commons the speech makes no difference to any outcome there. Here, the speech is the political act. I'm not saying it matters all the time, of course it doesn't, but far more than in the Commons. When we were in opposition I can think of four or five votes that have been won or lost in the chamber on the speech and the wind-up. On Incapacity benefit we got extra money; I actually got Tebbit voting against his own government with me on disability. We did that in the wind-up. The chamber was crowded, people standing at benches, and you have got seven minutes to come back for the opposition and try and defeat the government. You've got to do it in a way that's not too aggressive, and makes it possible for people to speak and be inclusive. You've got to go for issues that don't spend too much money, because the government can't allow that to happen. You've got to go for issues that haven't got a high, ideological profile. You've got to go for Tuesday afternoon between 4 o'clock and 5.30. If we do those things and get your troops in, including Tory troops, you could, when we were in opposition, with 70 votes, beat a government with two hundred. Monday, they're still coming in, Thursdays they're going home, and Wednesday afternoons there are general debates. So, Tuesday is the best time to keep them. By 5.30 the City vote comes in, and they haven't listened. Before 4 o'clock they're still coming in.

Lady Hollis, Labour

Whatever people say about this alleged, vast, inbuilt majority - which on paper there might be but, in terms of those who turn up, there is not - it's up to you as minister to try and make sure that you not only keep your own people on side, but also make sure you can bring in a reasonable number of cross-benchers. All the cross-benchers plus the then official opposition and the Liberals could easily defeat the government, particularly if a lot of the government's supporters thought the government's case was weak. When the division bell went they either sat on their hands or stayed in the library.

Lord Henley, Conservative

One of the problems that I've seen in my period here over 13 years, is the difference between the public perception of the House of Lords as a good place, largely fuelled by seeing it on television, and the reality which is that it is an intensely political place. If one looks at what happened over the last 18 years of Conservative government, yes, there were occasions when the House of Lords defeated the Conservative Government, but it had no effect on government policy. On virtually every occasion those defeats of the Conservative Government were overturned in the House of Commons and didn't see the light of day. So it was a sort of nine day propaganda victory which had no effect.

Lord Monkswell, Labour

Less than four years into the Thatcher government, we'd already got the message that there were things we could do in the Lords that nobody else could. She was so powerful in other ways at the time of the Falklands war before the 1983 election. There was nobody willing to oppose her. In the Lords we were gaining self-confidence after the 1979 defeat. My Chief Whip was Tom Ponsonby, Labour, and I'd known him on the GLC and he was very much a consensus politician and unwilling to challenge the traditions of the House. So when I suggested to him that we should do ambushes, that we should tell people to come back at nine o'clock at night he was very reluctant to do that. But I persuaded him to do it and it became a tactic that we used quite sparingly, not more than four or five times. We put the fear of God into the Tories. The older peers loved it. They thought this was great game and they would crowd into the chamber afterwards to hear the result. We never lost. It was always successful because intelligence between the parties is not that great here. We won because we did things in the evening, when the Tories had let people go. They kept a House, which is thirty, but they didn't have people staying along to vote. We didn't do it with crossbench support because cross-benchers go home in the evening. We occasionally did it with Liberal support but not always even then. So, it was a straight tactical ploy. There was nothing specifically political about it. It was just a little bit more aggressive than we'd been in the past. Tom liked, as we now like in government, to have agreements about everything in advance. The Tories, on the whole, cooperate with that.

Lord McIntosh, Labour

We were masters of the ambush, cowboys and indians. Very rarely, but every now and again, in the Commons, you would win by an ambush. In the House of Lords, you could only win by an ambush. I'm proud to say that in the last year of being the Chief Whip, in February and March 1997, we carried four amendments against four bills, which buggered up the government timetable. The government timetable was predicated on getting certain bills out but the Police Bill, the Scottish Crime and Punishment Bill, the Education Bill, we passed amendments up here which meant that our colleagues in the Commons could negotiate and improve them. That was ambush and colleagues enjoyed it.

I remember Eddie Shackleton writing me a note after an ambush saying, "Well done, Ted. It was just like old times. I felt I was back in the Commons again." You got a bit of excitement. There's nothing better for a Chief Whip in reporting the figures to the House, to turn round to his colleagues after you've declared the result and seeing 70 or 80 grinning Labour faces, all if not ecstatic, very pleased with themselves, because they've made an effort, they've made arrangements, they've stayed 'til the morning.

One night, we decided the only way we could win was to collaborate with the Liberals and to have votes after 12 o'clock at night. In the Commons you grumble but you sit around until the vote. Alexander Hesketh was the Tory Chief Whip and Geoff Tordoff and I calculated that after midnight they would have less than 60. So we planned to get more than 70 there after midnight.

We called a vote at 12.10 and we won, 78 to 52. Then the Tory Chief Whip was very, very angry and threatened all sorts of consequences if we kept the troops there. I said to him, in effect, "you can do what you like", and we called another vote and we won. And the great joy was Emily Blanche, as the Minister for Education, had then to concede eight amendments. So we won two victories and got eight concessions, truly as a result of 78, 80 and   sometimes 90 year olds coming along. That was a great lesson to me on the stick-ability of Labour people who knew all they could do was to be there. But they were there.

Lord Graham, Labour

If it was done by an ambush rather than a sort of genuine defeat, where obviously the whole House was against, you would reverse that in the Commons without a backward glance. It's the ones where you'd actually lost the argument that you would probably keep in the House of Commons. So it was nice fun and games as far as the Labour Party was concerned. A good tease but actually not very effective. The thing that is effective in this House is if you win the argument you very often win the vote. Or persuade the government to give way on the floor of the House. They do that in the Commons too, but it is a thing here where you more often have people who know what they're talking about because most people have a principal job outside the House and politics is their secondary one. Therefore you do have people with an more up to date knowledge in this House.

Lord Denham, Conservative

In my time, I would have thought I stage-managed about 15 ambushes and 14 of them we won. Only one we lost by careless talk. Some of our colleagues, they're either deaf or they think their colleague is deaf. You got things like, going up to a colleague in the library and saying, "What time is the ambush tonight?" and, of course, the other Tories look around and say, "What's going on?" You get things like somebody coming through for an 8.30 vote and saying to the doorkeeper in a loud voice, "Has the vote taken place yet?" And, of course, the Tories leaving say, "What's this about a vote?" By and large, we would have to apply subterfuge and it works, but human nature being what it is, sometimes we were let down. Latterly, I never put anything in writing, because one of the letters I sent out told people the time of the vote. That got into the hands of a gossip columnist and it appeared on the Sunday before a Monday night vote. It said "Poor old Lord Graham is bringing in his troops in order to vote at 8.30. What a pity they're wasting their time because the government now knows." On the Monday, all the Tories came through with a big grin and said, "You're rumbled, we know you've got a vote tonight." I said, "I don't know what you're talking about." It turned out we had the vote and won by 30. The Tories refused to believe that we would have persisted with the vote by the fact that they knew we were going to have it.

I could honestly say that it was enjoyable and it was worth the pain, and we sweated. The number of times my colleagues came to me in the course of a night saying, "They know we are going to have a vote, we may as well go home." My job was to step in and say, "Look, even if they do know, we've told people to come in, we're going to have a vote, and we're going to win." "How do you know we're going to win?" I said, "Because they're stupid. They won't believe we can win."

Lord Graham, Labour

We wouldn't plot with them in any detailed, structured way. But I knew both Tom Ponsonby, Labour, and Ted Graham extremely well and used to look at the opportunities that there were. And we would exchange our views on what we were going to do. You would find at 9.30 at night a lot of opposition peers would suddenly appear from nowhere. There have been many issues on which the two parties have overlapped over the years. We are or were both left of centre radical parties. Whether the Labour Party still is is another matter but, obviously, there's a lot of common interest. There's a fair amount of lobby fodder there, particularly on Conservative benches of course, because they've got so many. I remember on one occasion we defeated the government and I said to the government Chief Whip, 'You made a mistake today'. He said, 'What's that?' I said, 'You let your people carry on into the chamber and listen to the debate.' They should keep them in the library.

Lord Tordoff, Liberal Democrat

You've got to appeal to people and be sensible. I worked out that in three sessions a year - that's from October to Christmas, Christmas to Easter, Easter to Summers - in each one of those times, I would have an ambush. But only three. That was all. The other thing I've learned is, you call people for a vote at 9.30 and you win it, by 82 to 37. And your colleagues say, "Vote again". The great man who made his reputation was John MacKay who came from the Commons and was a political animal. There was one night on Transport when Stanley Clinton-Davis, and Denis Howell were haggling and they came to a situation where we were going to win three times, and we had the numbers. We won the first and second one, and we mucked up calling the vote on the third one, which allowed MacKay to get up and fillibuster. He was a past master at it. After half an hour, our people were as sick as dogs. I made the decision then, never ever try to win more than one vote at a time, because colleagues are quite willing to come along at 12.10, providing they get away at 12.20. But they're not in the business like at the Commons where they'll stop as long as they can.

Lord Graham, Labour

When I was in opposition, one year we had four social security bills, including the Disability Bill, and I could win amendments here that we hadn't a hope in hell of winning down the Commons. You could never get a victory in the Commons or defeat the government. The trick up here was not only to get the victory but to get enough Tories attached to your numbers so it wasn't overturned down the other end. Trying to build that network, trying to get really worthwhile things like pension shares were actually some of the most useful things I've done in my life.

It could only be done in this sort of forum and it could only be done because we don't have a Speaker, because we do have cross-benchers and because the whip runs fairly lightly, and it all takes place on the floor of the House. Therefore the chamber, not the committee room, not the tea room or the smoking room is the focus of political life. If you decide to take the House seriously, and you're a fool not too, you could actually do a lot of good things here which you can't possibly do down the other end.

Lady Hollis, Labour

I can get politically quite tense. The Greater London Council Bill was a great time and we had some fun with the Poll Tax here as well. Those are the sorts of things that stand out. But even on a day to day basis, the Railways Bill for instance, quite a lot went into that to get protection for the Railwaymen's pension fund. In the end, we managed to get the government to change the Bill. I'm not saying that the pensions would necessarily have been threatened but, nevertheless, we felt we had to put protection into the Bill that wasn't there and we got it. So it was quite exciting.

Lord Tordoff, Liberal Democrat

In an awful lot of issues you have right on your side but you still don't win them in opposition. On the women's pensions issue I worked very hard. I chose some Tory women who count in the Tory Party and coaxed them to come into an alliance with me; I worked the cross-benchers to get them, and the Lib Dems. So I put together an alliance. Several of them were women. I ended up in some cases having to draft their speeches but you had to do it in a way that made it possible to talk about the good sense of the House. The moment you start doing ding-dongs or "Labour's good, Tory is bad", you've lost the House. You've wasted your time. Cross-benchers don't want to know.

There they sit in judgement, Nobel Prizewinners, Vice Chancellors, former Law Lords, Bishops, College of Surgeons, distinguished writers, people who have got their own minds. They're politically alert, but not party politically identified. You've got to persuade them. If you intend to win, you've got to get two-thirds or three-quarters of the cross-benchers with you, and if you haven't got three-quarters of them with you you probably don't deserve to win. I was doing the big Pensions Bill, in the aftermath of Maxwell's scandal and we then tried to get divorce property settlements built into pensions. Later we had the Matrimonial Bill and I then tried to get pensions built into the Divorce bill. I did it in two steps, and we went part of the way on the first one so we could win the first and bank it. I could come back to it, having got, I hoped, a half-way educated House on the second bill. But it was made possible because of the support all round the House, including the Tory benches. The key thing was getting things like the Mother's Union members writing in to the Bishops. They came on side and said it was OK as a Christian to recognise that divorce and clean breaks happen and you've got to have fairness of settlement. You had to permit Tory people not to come in behind the government case and find a language and discourse which they could speak.

Lady Hollis, Labour

The Tory Party up here has nearly 500 people to vote. If you forget about people who are in the hospices and can't get up and so forth the Labour Party, which received an enormous majority in 1997, can turn out a maximum of about 92. The Opposition can defeat us on absolutely anything it wants to. For them, the decision is only which amendments shall we beat them on. Then they have no problem, they only have to get in one in three of their people, and they get a massive majority. They have now defeated us 20 times. If they defeat us three more times, that will be the greatest number of defeats in the last quarter of the century. But it's not just a question of defeat. Because they can do it when they like, at any time, and they do do it, we have to turn out our troops the whole time. The House of Lords doesn't lead any easy short life like the House of Commons. We actually work very long hours. I was here in the chamber at 1.15 this morning as a minister, and the other ministers were all here. They're in the office at 8.30 and they're expected to do all their ministerial jobs, and we were in until after midnight twice the week before the recess. Four days a week, we have three-line whips, so the whole Labour team is here, including men of 70 or 80. After midnight, men of 80 odd, just sitting here, waiting.

Lord Donoughue, Labour

In government we have authority without power up in this place. At the moment, the Tories have clearly decided to observe the Salisbury convention, more or less, but to inflict one to three defeats on each bill. They ration themselves because they clearly aren't going to break the Salisbury convention.

There's an understanding. We all speak the language of keeping the show on the road. The usual channels keep going whatever happens. They will work out one to two defeats and try to make sure it doesn't happen in committee. We make sure it happens in report. So it can be overturned down the bottom end. But sometimes, and particularly in the areas I've been working on, which have been the lone parent business, and backdating of social security where there would have been political difficulties for the government to overturn defeats here down at the other end, then I've had to do some foot work. So far so good. We still have a long way to go. I still have a third reading to go which I could be defeated on. But if people listen to you, if they think you know what you're talking about, and if they think you're worth listening to and they like you, and this sort of thing, then we should do it.

Lady Hollis, Labour

The House of Lords was the only opposition that the Conservative Government ever had. I was the Conservative Chief Whip for much of that time, so I know very well how much trouble the House of Lords gave to the government. There are many examples of the House of Lords making the Conservative Government change its mind. Now that the boot is on the other foot it is the Labour Government that object so much to any advice that is given by the House of Lords. Remember that the power of this second chamber is relatively limited. All we're asking the House of Commons to do is to think again on one or two issues. Yet that seems to give the government a great deal of trouble.

Lord Strathclyde, Conservative

It's not changed an enormous amount with the change of government. First of all, the beautiful, territorial battles which affect us - the Liberal Democrats - so much, because the Tories are so cramped on their benches and the cross-benchers, were actually better organised. That's because they ceded one part of their traditional territory, but occupied another one on the Government's side and are there in very large numbers for prayers so that no one can take their seats. Liberals are not very good at prayers so there are very few and there's an increasing risk that Tory peers will move over into Liberal Democrat benches. Labour on the other hand, were quite cramped, especially on the front bench, but now sit there comfortably, for the moment, and have no problem finding a place to sit.

Initially it was interesting to see how people had to get used to their new roles. I remember a government minister in our question period asking questions, and having to be reminded that he was now minister and that he had to give answers. Similarly, it still happens that ex-ministers start making statements and have to be reminded they are now in opposition. It's a transitional period in which some of the now, opposition peers, have more information about subjects than some of our government peers.

But the main change is quite a pleasing one. If a government is in power for too long it has all sorts of hang-ups, and there are certain, simple questions to which it's got used to giving the evasive answers, which are so boring. Now, suddenly, theirs are easy and spontaneous answers, like the Gulf War Syndrome, or particular asylum cases or whatever. At least for a period one gets fresh and direct answers for which they sometimes lead the minister into trouble, which is refreshing and one of the aspects of change which are so elementary for democracy.

Lord Dahrendorf, Liberal Democrat

When you get into opposition all the obvious things change. No car, no Rolls Royce. I was lucky enough to be served by the Cabinet Office, marvellous, never been better served. And charming unassuming people too. Very good eggs. It's a pity they aren't better organised. Two things struck me. One was that firstly, I didn't expect it and, secondly, I didn't mind very much because I have another life. I'm an amateur politician. If I was sacked by William Hague tomorrow I genuinely wouldn't mind. I'd go back to my life and have a hell of a good time. I've got things to do. But my colleagues had suffered a serious bereavement. They were in mourning, in shock. They'd lost their wife, husband, in many cases more. Mainly my Cabinet colleagues, I think. It was also true among some of my people here. The ones who were most committed.

It was more difficult here because Thomas and I are the only opposition people who are paid. So my front-bench do it for love. Expenses are fixed, quite rightly, and I always try and emphasise to the pay review body that we were on the side of meanness of expenses of the House of Lords. Labour wanted us to be much more generous. If you're too generous it doesn't look good so long as you remain an amateur House. So they're doing this for love and I did actually persuade Ken Clarke to offer either some ring-fenced Short money for the House of Lords. They thought Christmas had come but it was pretty obvious to all of us I think we were going to lose the election. It did occur to me that in opposition I would need a little money. If we were really badly beaten our Short money allocation down the corridor would be much less generous, and we really would be in trouble. So I recruited one of the best of the politicos in the No. 10 Policy Unit of the Major Government. I said, "Do you want to come and work for me afterwards". He said, "Yes". He's next door. He basically is the engine room of the Opposition.

It was difficult. I'd never been in opposition before. We need to learn how to organise ourselves. I was very keen that we shouldn't reshuffle responsibilities until I'd seen who was good at what, who had the time. A lot had to find jobs, part-time. Very few of my people have independent means, almost none of them. So I waited until the Autumn before making a judgement. Meanwhile, it was very interesting seeing former ministers shadowing their own departments. You could see them saying, and I used to find myself saying, "I remember that problem, it was a real sod. Would I have done the same as this minister has in my place? Probably yes". So you go softly. But knowledge of the department becomes less of an advantage as time goes on. That's the time to reshuffle, I think.

Lord Cranborne, Conservative

It's a traumatic experience to cross the side of the House. You're sitting in a different place, and particularly after the defeat of May 1st 1997 which was of a quite different order than the defeat of 1974 had been. I think that the difference is the proposal of the Labour Party to abolish the right of hereditary peers to sit and vote in the House.

Lady Young, Conservative

There is a bit of a rearguard action going on at the moment. Something that I have tried to encourage is that, when we do defeat the goverment, we should try and make it the House of Lords as a whole not just the Tories. So that it's seen to be a reasonable issue above party, involving people of all parties and none. That is quite a sensible ploy because it's the sort of thing the House of Lords should stand for anyway.

Lord Cranborne, Conservative

After the election when we first came back somebody asked me how are the Tories reacting now that they've been defeated. I had to point out that in the House of Lords they hadn't been defeated. They are still there, and they came back as if there was no change. Because the Tories in the House of Lords have this inbuilt majority - they could defeat the government any time they felt like it - and it's been intriguing watching the way that that majority is being used.

On the amendments that they put to the referendum bills for devolution, they picked aspects that have a resonance in the country, so that people would say "Oh yes, that seems fairly sensible" - like having referendums on the same day. I suspect that that is the way in which they will carry on. They will pick their targets very carefully, they are not stupid. And they will defeat the Labour Government on issues that they can stand up in public about and say, "We thought this was quite reasonable", but underlying it there is, as you say, a war of attrition against a Labour Government.

Lord Monkswell, Labour

At the end of the day it is impotent but it can turn quite nasty and it can mean that the government is seriously embarrassed by their timetable being disrupted. So far it hasn't happened seriously but I think we're moving into an era where probably ,in the next 12 months, there will be more problems and parliamentary timetables being messed up by the House of Lords.

Lord Whitty, Labour

Abolition is going to be the real problem because even if we get agreement with Cranborne and co. which, I suppose, is less likely, we must expect the next session for the hereditary backbenchers to take it out on us in other ways, which they certainly can with the rules in this House. People coming from the Commons can't believe that all the possibilities for disruption, which would be used in the Commons, exist here and aren't used. That's the fundamental difference. So whether they really hate us, as I'm sure they will next year, it's going to get very rough indeed.

Lord McIntosh, Labour

I'm here for votes, for the three-line whips, 3.30 every day because it's not only the danger of being defeated, the biggest worry is of losing the quorum, losing the House. You have to be 30. I was here at 1 o'clock last night. Why? Although we knew that only half a dozen Tories were here, all they had to do was move a division and then not vote, and if we didn't have 30, the business would end. Because the programme's so packed, there isn't a day free. If you lose some hour's business, half a day's business, and you have to come back, there isn't another day to come back. So we're here into the early hours, to make sure that we don't lose a vote. That would be bad, because then the Commons has got to overturn it, but worse would be to lose the business.

Lord Donoughue, Labour

The House of Lords is full of people of independent mind. This business about the Conservative majority in the House of Lords is a bit of a myth. On a normal working day the Conservative peers and Labour peers and crossbenchers have a very equal attendance. The Conservative majority can be called in, but on a normal working day it's not there. So this overwhelming need to change things is not necessarily a fact.

Lord Colwyn, Conservative

Whether that discipline will remain as tight in government is another matter. Already we've seen considerable disquiet on the student loans, and on one or two other matters, like some aspects of the Crime and Disorder Bill. A lot of Labour backbenchers are not happy. They think it's following too much in the Michael Howard agenda. There are a number of Labour backbenchers who have considerable unease about student loans. How far they will push that will be another matter, but certainly when we were in government, there were always a lot of people prepared to be difficult. In my years in Social Security I used to dread seeing amendments down in Lady Faithfull's name, when we had social security bills . You can have up to four names on any amendment and there would be a group of three others coming from other sides of the House, so she could argue this was an all-party amendment. It was very difficult to win under those circumstances.

Lord Henley, Conservative

You can defeat the government with the help of the cross-benchers or the Liberals, but not with the inherent majority. This is a great misconception. I think the Tebbit amendment to the Northern Ireland Sentences Bill is an absolutely classic case in point. In the House there was an overwhelming Tory majority for supporting the Tebbit Bill. There was a whip on. I was under strict instructions from the Shadow Cabinet that we should support Tebbit. And we had a big turnout. Tebbit got 150 something votes, one of the highest Tory turnouts of the session. Which shows actually, how few Tories had read it and actually turned up.

There is a difference between the nominal strength and the actual strength. Very difficult for Labour to understand and I absolutely agree with them. I think it's an anomaly that has to be corrected in any case. But the fact of the matter is, on the strongest whip we ever put out Thomas never got more than 200. That was the only three-line whip we ever issued and most of the blighters didn't turn out or abstained. The cross-benchers particularly, said we believe the government, when the government says the Tebbit amendment breaks the agreement. However sympathetic, they were not prepared to do that. So the truth of the matter is that unless Dennis Carter the Labour Whip can get his troops here, which increasingly he can't because dinner in Islington is obviously a stronger pull than his whip, we need to be sure of the support of quite a few cross-benchers. Not the bishops, I don't worry about them. With that sort of support, we could certainly win a lot more often than we do, a lot more often. But it would be a mistake

Lord Cranborne, Conservative

They can defeat us any time they want to. And they don't need to have an ambush. Their difficulty at the moment is to stop people going into the Lobby against us and defeating us far more frequently than would be popular.

Lord McIntosh, Labour

You need to change your way of thinking. If you're me in this job you have to regard yourself as a sort of guerrilla leader. The most important thing is realising it's a long, long road. And that apparent victory is not actually necessarily the objective. You've got to wear down the other side and that's going to make it very difficult to maintain the morale of your own troops. So, I think you have to change your attitude and mind a little and try and look to them as though you know precisely what you're doing, particularly when you don't. Give them confidence. But above all, jokes. Make it fun. Make them laugh. Make it seem more fun to be here than out earning a crust. So you don't have any boxes and you don't work the same hours but it's a different kind of effort. In many ways it's more fun. You're highly reliant on yourself. I'm very lucky having Thomas, who's a great Chief Whip.

Lord Cranborne, Conservative

There's no question of asking large numbers of people, who don't normally attend, to come. I think that would be wrong. I think it was just as wrong to get them to attend. I think that there are very reasonable points which will have to be sent back to the Commons on devolution and all that.

What makes it difficult is that in a way the House of Lords suits the Labour Government more than it suits the Conservative Government. If the Conservative Government was defeated by the House of Lords, it's obviously made a grade one boo-boo. And it actually ought to pay attention. But even then, they didn't all the time, especially when Jack Straw and Michael Howard got together. But if it's a Labour Government defeat in the House of Lords, they just say poo-poo, silly Dukes, who don't represent anything. So they need pay no attention to the argument. The Tories hope, because of their strength, to get away with no argument. When they do, they actually have to pay more attention to it. I want a system whereby both sides have to give attention to the argument and listen to it because the House is talking sense. In it's present composition, it lacks that authority, and I want it to get its authority back.

Earl of Onslow, Conservative

The Shadow Cabinet suddenly discovers the only people who can cause trouble for the government are the Tories in the House of Lords. So they start trying to micro-manage you. They are peeved about the House of Lords. They're only thinking about tomorrow's political advantage and they don't recognise that we have to think a little bit longer and how would it look if we managed to make an alliance with the cross-benchers, which is not difficult, and roll over the government about 40 times a week? It would not only devalue the currency but I think the public, quite rightly, would be slightly irritated. So we've got to walk this tightrope here of not devaluing the currency but at the same time not letting your muscles atrophy because people are going to say what's the point of it? So you have to box clever.

I had a very entertaining conversation with Peter Carrington the other day: Peter; "Hello Robert, how are you? Are the Shadow Cabinet telling you what to do yet?" "Er, yes". "What do you say to them?" I say, "Well, I'll do my best to follow instructions, and then do precisely what I think is right". "Good", he said, "that's what I did too".

Lord Cranborne, Conservative

CHAPTER EIGHT

Back to Basics

IN October 1967 a Labour Government, with a majority big enough to do whatever it wanted, announced in its second Queen's Speech a bill "to reduce the present powers of the House of Lords and eliminate its present hereditary basis". It was introduced. It didn't do the job. 31 years later, in November 1998, another Labour Government with an even bigger majority announced its bill "to remove the right of hereditary peers to sit and vote in the House of Lords". This time it was based on a manifesto commitment, unlike 1967.

Neither government had decided exactly what to do; an unfortunate failure, for that is the difficulty in discussing the Lords. To reform some of it is to reform all of it. The Wilson Government of 1967 promised consultations. Early the following year an all-party group agreed to take away the right of the hereditaries to vote but allowing them to attend, ask questions, and sit on committees. These proposals were accepted by the lords themselves by 251 to 56. In 1998 the Blair Government promised a new system of appointment for life peers, then a Royal Commission to "speedily" bring forward proposals for reform to make the Lords "more democratic and representative".

The Lords of the 60s reacted negatively. When the Commons passed an Order approving United Nations Sanctions against Rhodesia and its UDI, the Lords rejected it by 193-184. 30 years later they reacted ever more strongly and more often, yet also more sensibly. The Blair Government was defeated 39 times in its first session. Its European Elections Bill was thrown out five times, on each occasion by the hereditaries for a majority of the life peers voted for it, while a Commons decision, taken on a free vote to lower the homosexual age of consent, was plucked out of the Crime Bill and thrown out. When the government tried to adopt the Lloyd George routine and whip up populist hostility to privilege and a permanent Tory majority in the Lords, it naturally got a programmed reaction from its own people, even though Labour MPs, by the 90s, were more elitist, less populist, and ready to compromise. Yet the attack produced no wider resonance. Perhaps the Blair Government was too associated with other forms of privilege. Although most people were happy to abolish hereditaries, even if they didn`t regard the matter as urgent, the majority thought the Lords were right on homosexuality and European elections. Moreover, try as the government might to portray the Lords as a Tory-dominated obstruction to Labour and one dedicated, as Balfour had put it, to ensuring that "in power or in opposition" the Tory Party should continue to control Britain's destiny, in fact most defeats were minimal, easily borne and readily reversed. They were inconveniences, not roadblocks, to a government with an unprecedented majority. The European Elections Bill caused real problems but that was mainly because the government was anxious to face down the Lords on the issue and win a measure its own MPs supported only reluctantly.

The similarities between 1967 and 1998 are so striking because while both reforms were simple proposals, they opened up far wider issues, as second chamber reform always must. To broach it is to open up a can of second chamber worms as the unsolved questions of powers, composition, role and the relationship with the people and their representatives - the Commons - emerge. Indeed, even the basic issue of the hereditaries posed problems. Should they be turned out of their own club? Should some stay on or be allowed to speak but not vote; should those who work hardest, or sit in the protected game reserve of the cross-benches, keep their seats and role, and should the onstayers stay in their own right or be reincarnated as life peers after a change of credit cards and a bit of fuss from Garter King of Arms, possibly with reduced fees for batch creations? These problems caused hereditary hopes to spring arthritic, if not eternal.

Over all these questions hovers the central issue. Would abolition of hereditaries be, or end up becoming faute de mieux, the only and insufficient, reform? Or would it be the prelude to a real reform, or the trigger to "big bang", leading to a genuinely new Second Chamber? As New Labour moved to New Lords, old and existing ones were obsessed by basic problems which they had thought more about than anyone else.

If there's a groundswell of questioning, then the Lords will collapse. As long as there isn't such a groundswell and people appreciate that it's a dotty British institution which works, why fiddle with it? That's basically my view. I also think that if you begin to ask questions, it'll unravel. I worry a bit about unnecessary changes when there are so many important things but I gather the Prime Minister shares our views so he'll not put something on the agenda which is strictly unnecessary. I was delighted to be appointed. I've only been there for four years. I wouldn't have accepted it if I wanted to change it out of recognition, and I have not discovered anything which makes me a great reformer.

Lord Dahrendorf, Liberal Democrat

In some ways we're throwing away everything traditional. The monarchy is very unpopular at the moment, and let's get rid of judges having wigs. The House of Lords comes into that. There isn't any feeling of value in retaining traditions whereas, in the past, tradition was something Britain had always been quite good at. While other countries completely changed their constitution, there was something about Britain we wanted to try and retain, some of the tradition. That was a good thing. But I notice that that's going and I suppose the argument really for keeping the hereditary peers is that it's historical.

Lord Glasgow, Liberal Democrat

I am and still remain a firm adherent to the philosophy of Nye Bevan, "The language of priorities is the religion of Socialism". When I think of the measures that can be passed with the large majority, I can think of a thousand priorities before I can get myself involved in what is ultimately a quite pointless constitutional exercise. It's one which the Commons itself would not, ultimately, wear anyway, and the abolition of the right to vote by hereditary peers is really more symbolic than substantial. I'd leave things as they are. If we tackle, thoroughly, poverty in the United Kingdom, if we tackle effectively the fact that the bottom 40% are at the poverty level by European standards, if we make a proper health service with a proportion of GDP devoted to it, then OK, let's come back to it. If we do all these vital things then by all means, if we've got a bit of spare time then shove it in. But to make it a priority issue is to allow it to smokescreen for session after session, because believe me, the Commons and the Lords amongst themselves, will argue interminably about this, and you've still got to have a speakers conference anyway to deal with the damn thing. It all acts as a smokescreen for lack of action in the things that really matter.

Lord Bruce, Labour

If it ain't broke don't fix it. But, anyway, they want to fix something so I think we should take it very carefully apart, look at it, see what works, what doesn't work and see what we want to go ahead with, and there should be a composite plan before anything else is done. But simply kicking out the hereditary peers for no better reason than that they had rather nice parents doesn't seem to me a very sound idea.

Lady Strange, Conservative

I've always been a unicameralist. When I actually got here, I discovered that whatever people might have thought about the House of Lords, once they got here, they were rather in favour of it continuing. I didn't change my mind. I still haven't. I used to be an ignorant unicameralist. I'm now a very well informed unicameralist. I remember that in the run up to the 1983 election, we had our party meetings every Thursday. What do I answer when people say, "What are you doing in the House of Lords when your party's in favour of abolishing it?" I stood up and said that I saw no problem whatsoever. You're here because it's here, and there are things to be done while it's still here. And Barbara Wootton drew herself up to her four foot, nine, and said, "I agree with Andrew, I'm a single chamber girl myself". Which was rather nice of her.

Lord McIntosh, Labour

The people couldn't give a stuff about the House of Lords, not a stuff. They don't know anything about what we do. We are very badly represented, we don't market ourselves at all. Occasionally, they'll see us on television and when they do they think the peers are asleep because they are leaning up against the speakers in the red benches by the microphones. But those who occasionally come here, say, "Gosh the level of the debate is incredible. How good it is and we're so glad there is a House of Lords". Foreigners come to London and say, you're "cotton-picking crazy". I've had them from the Canadian Senate, I've had them from France, so why do we want to do away with it, that's my first point? Don't reform it. Secondly if you do reform it, for God's sake don't throw the baby out with the bathwater. The worse thing you could do is shove in another 57 peers like the last 57 you shoved in. They've all come in loosely into two camps, ones that never shut up and ones that never attend.

Lady O'Cathain, Conservative

When I first came into the House of Lords some 12 years ago, there was a distinction between members of the House of Lords who had been members of the House of Commons before, and those that hadn't. Over the last three or four years that distinction has fallen away and a new distinction between lifers and hereditaries has come in which wasn't significant some years ago. So the political scene changes and when I first came in I suppose I had a principled view, like many people in the Labour and Trade Union movement, that the House of Lords should be abolished. But one of the problems was that on the day I came in, in January 1985, the House of Lords was televised for the first time and since then, this has been seen by the British public as being a good thing.

Lord Monkswell, Labour

As a second set of minds this House of Lords might as well do it as any other House of Lords. If I was in complete charge and I wanted to do something with the House of Lords I wouldn't muck about doing anything about the hereditary peers, I would cut the problem of delay. I would assess whether I could get away with abolishing delays so they couldn't get away with delaying bills at all. If we throw out a bill and it goes back and we have to use the Parliament Act, we lose 12 months. That's the power of the House of Lords. If we could get rid of that delay, make it six months, make it three months, there's no problem.

Lord McCarthy, Labour

The king's minister has actually nicked all the king's power. Tony Blair is actually the most powerful man since Oliver Cromwell. He's a wartless Oliver Cromwell. He's got total, complete power. It's bad for anybody to have that amount of power because that gives too much power to the Mandelsons, the Hagues, whoever it may be. I'm not making a party political point. I'm just making an old-fashioned weak balance of power point.

So you could have a slight counter-balance. But it can't be composed solely of hereditary peers. First of all, I'd increase the number of people who are there by their position on the judges and the bishops' row. I would certainly keep some power of appointment. I would make lots of professions and people elect them among themselves. I would keep, for historical reasons, some of the hereditary peers, on a self-elected basis. And I would have one-fifth elected in a totally different way, and nominated peers. I wouldn't want to take away totally the power of patronage. But the idea of the House of Lords being totally nominated is an appalling idea. When people say, we'll just abolish the hereditary peers and come up with something later, I say to myself, Ha, ha, ha, that's the sort of excuse someone gave at school for not knowing one's Latin. That's not going to wash. I know you don't want your legislation mucked about but I think the more everybody's legislation is mucked about the better. I think it is right that people should be able to say, "I'm not sure you've got this right, please think again". If we get much more into the habit of thinking like that, I think we would have a much better system of legislation. I am a whig in that sense; I like checks and balances.

Earl of Onslow, Conservative

I should think that probably for the last four generations members of my family have been asked how it feels to be the Salisbury that ends it all. I think we've viewed that with a certain amount of equanimity. After all Prime Minister Salisbury himself was the first man seriously to suggest reforming the House of Lords because he believed in a strong upper chamber, and his descendants have always felt the same way.

The difficulty with the hereditary peerage is that it's fine so long as they have power. People respect power. I think there is a curious rule which might say that you know when an institution is becoming weak, because people feel able to attack it with impunity. I'm sure that's why Lloyd George felt able to attack the House of Lords. He recognised that it's time had come and gone. So if you're going to have an institution that works I think it has to have the authority to function.

Lord Cranborne, Conservative

I would like to see us having rather more authority than we do now. One of the days that really stick in my mind is the last day of rail privatisation. We knew perfectly well the government was wrong. John Painton who had the amendments is one of the most courageous peers alive. We chose to back off because we don't believe we have the legitimacy to make really major challenges to the Commons. Even when we know they're needed. We saw the same thing over the Football Spectators Bill in 1989. Very often we've got the ball at our feet and we see an open goal, but we don't shoot because we believe we're not allowed to win. If the House gets reformed, I would like to see it - assuming it has rather more authority - check the Commons where the Commons have made a muck of things.

Lord Russell, Liberal Democrat

The value of the hereditary peers is that we're not professional. We have a sense of amateurishness in the absolute, best sense of the word. I think there is a traditional sense of duty. I think they do care. Certainly a lot of us voted quite persistently against the last government. You've only got to see young Freyburg on war pensions. Believe it or not, if you behave half reasonably, people do seem to think you're of some use. Most of them give back to their community. All right, it is on the whole a rural community, because it fits easily into a rural scene. It fits less well into South Kensington and obviously less well into, for want of a better word, working class suburbs.

Earl of Onslow, Conservative

You have a second chamber which doesn't challenge the House of Commons as the sovereign chamber but insists on its right to give advice, to look at and revise legislation and in the last analysis to say to the House of Commons, "well we really think you must consider this for another year". I think that we've struck, in a peculiar way, a reasonable balance. If we go any further than that and if we say that we want an elected House of Lords by universal suffrage then it will demand power and eventually it will get it. If you have a division of powers in the sort of constitution we have, that could be difficult and I think the House of Commons in the past has been sensible enough to realise that. Whether it could be sensible enough in the future I can't say. What you'd be doing by throwing out the hereditaries is throwing out any independent voice there is. First of all you increase the power of the Prime Minister through patronage and instead of having a diverse House you will have a House of people who are dependent upon the patronage of somebody else. What you have is the biggest quango in the country and I'm not at all sure that that is a valid reform. The other thing is if you can take the vote away from the hereditaries somebody else can give it back, so you haven't dealt with it.

It's not a problem of them being called in from the shires. That really isn't true. There are twice as many hereditaries as there are appointed so that if you're having a vote it's almost inevitable there's going to be a hell of a lot of hereditary peers there. The other thing about the hereditaries coming down from the backwoods is a lot of them wouldn't be seen dead in the place. They don't like it, they don't want to be here. If you're going to reform the House of Lords you can't do it in isolation. To fiddle with hereditaries probably at the most difficult time when we have a lot of things to do will be counter-productive. It's better to have a proper reform than to have a piecemeal reform which might prove to be disastrous. You either need a speaker's conference or a Royal Commission to take as much time as necessary. The House of Lords has been here since 1230 at least, so there's no great rush to do it.

Lord Stoddart, Labour

In terms of actual power the House of Lords is much more powerful than the European Parliament, and in its own way, more democratic. This love/hate relationship between the Lords and the Commons exists because the House of Commons never wants anybody to challenge its ultimate authority to rule. Thereby it sets up a completely untenable position in relation to the Lords. If, for example, the Lords are made into an elected chamber - I don't care how elected, either as representing local authorities or with individual constituents, whatever it may be - once it challenged the House of Commons, the Commons wouldn't wear it. On the one hand it doesn't like the hereditary principle and on the other hand it wouldn't countenance the Lords challenging its ultimate power. That dilemma is one that they first of all have to solve.

Lord Bruce, Labour

If you think about 1968, the proposals had the support of both parties so in effect it had a majority just as big, if not bigger, than the Prime Minister commands at the moment. Yet it still fell apart in the Commons because there were enough in the Commons who did not like the proposals because they thought a strengthened Lords would mean a weaker Commons. The proposals back in 1968 were not that different from just removing hereditary peers, but I think still allows them to sit and speak, but not vote. I forget but I certainly wouldn't want to support such an idea that you could have second class members.

Lord Henley, Conservative

I honestly think that Blair is a control freak. I think he's mucking around with the constitution and he's like an "A" Level science student let loose with a nuclear bomb. This man is dangerous because of his inexperience and ignorance. He doesn't realise the importance of an independent element in Parliament. He fears it , rather as Lloyd George feared it. I think once he's got rid of the hereditaries, he'll be absolutely delighted not to put anything in their stead And that's very bad for parliament. It gives the government absolute power.

I'm being perfectly consistent about reform. When I was in government, I used to say to Major, "let's go for it now. Quite apart from it being a politically sensitive thing do to, it needs doing and you know it". He didn't really have the conviction to do it and he couldn't persuade anyone in the Cabinet to do it anyway. But it's an awful shame he didn't because I think we'd have done it better. The club-like atmosphere's fine but parliamentarians are a fairly clubbable lot anyway. Some of them are, and if they're the clubbable ones, they'll be clubbable whatever the second chamber. In the House of Lords, they go to the bars anyway. So, in a way it's a bit too cosy. I think I'd like something a little bit more muscular.

Lord Cranborne, Conservative

I don't care about the hereditary peers. On the whole they're quite good because a lot of young sons of aristocracy spend a few years in the House of Lords, though whether they'll do it in opposition I don't know. In office all the best people on the other side were undoubtedly hereditary peers because all the other buggers are broken down old has-beens from the Commons who've been sent here because she promised they could all go, and they never even came. They never turned up, they're absolutely useless - and when they do they just make speeches about their past. They're absolutely useless. But the professional hereditary peers are very useful. You'll never see Tebbit doing anything useful. They just make speeches.

Lord McCarthy, Labour

I look at the hereditary element. After 20 years I think I know all of them. Personally they are all very much of a muchness. You obviously get people who are of the very extreme right, with whom I have about as much sympathy as I would with Sir Oswald Mosley. They're here together with members that are really quite genial in their own way, some of them highly studious and some of them do a very good and detailed job of work. They and are in the Tory Party more or less by habit rather than by any deep political conviction. For them I think in the main it is a question of class. Social class determines very largely the composition of the Tory benches. On the Labour side we have exactly the same kind of thing. We've got some first class chaps. We have a number of people who really don't work frightfully hard, and we do have a number of people who perhaps, with some justification, regard the ending of their political career in the Lords as a more peaceful way of fulfilling the political ambitions of a lifetime. A sort of a quiet closing down. Loyal. They'll say anything you like, but they find it convenient to study rather less than is necessary to be part of a fully qualified legislature.

As to the hereditary side of it, it's very difficult to decide. In democratic theory of course to have hereditary peers is indefensible - yet when I look at the turn out of legislation (I'm talking apart from the highly contentious stuff) there's very little to choose in intellectual effort and intellectual attitude between one side or another - hereditary or life peer. I have known life peers, and I use the words "have known" so it doesn't have any present connotations that might be taken amiss, who quite frankly are dumb. Not through any personal defect but because, as they concede, their role in life has been rather a passive one. I could apply the same thing to the Tories.

There are some quite smart hereditary peers, and I can assure you from personal experience that the hereditary role of the 'Cecils' should not be underestimated. They are some of the smartest political operators under the sun. Some of the hereditary peers really knew their onions centuries ago and do show certain signs of the brilliance with which their ancestors have been attributed. Intellectually, I don't think you could say on the whole that a life peer is any more efficient or effective than an hereditary peer. The latter is the descendant of the past preferment, while life peers are the product of present preferment, so we both have the preferment behind the positions that we occupy. But in terms of parliamentary status I would hesitate to say that the life peers are any more efficient than the hereditary ones.

Lord Bruce, Labour

I think there is a need for some reform and I think perhaps they could stop the back-woodsmen coming in when there's a major vote, in other words restrict the voting to actual working peers, whether they're life or hereditary peers, rather than have people who they can call in. Calling in the back-woodsmen is what has brought the House of Lords into disrepute.

Countess of Mar, Cross-bencher

Being the son of your father and coming to the Lords is no worse than being a Prime Minister's favourite or a failed politician. I don't like the thought of losing all the youth. There have been some very good young men. Lindsey is one. Excellent. I remember one of his first speeches, getting up and saying, it might make a change to hear the younger generation's point of view. Well, that would go. I speak as an ex-whip. To say you can make them do what you want is a load of balony. They will do what they want to. Some of them, if you try and press them, will bend the other way just to do that to you. True, there have been, in the past, a great many more of them, but now, if the Opposition win too many divisions, it's very difficult. I think we try and make a stand when we feel it's really important for the country, in a totally unpartisan way, but what we think is the best for the country, and you've got some damn good hereditary peers in with the life peers. I just think it's a pity.

Lady Trumpington, Conservative

The hereditary peers run the place. The ethos of the administration of the place is by procedural and administrative committees which are dominated mainly by the hereditaries plus some lawyers. So, in reforming the place, we've actually got to look at the way we run things here. The ethos is a sort of 65-year old's public school. I think their main influence is on the ethos of the place rather than the procedure in the chamber or on the committees. By and large the life peers dominate the debate. There are a few hereditaries in the leadership of the Tories who are still strong but, in general, most of the Tory spokespeople are life peers, not hereditaries. So if you went through a list of people who contributed to debates, certainly main debates, the vast majority would be life peers, and you could lose the hereditaries with no damage at all.

Lord Whitty, Labour

My view is that an astonishing number of the House of Commons actually don't know about the real world because they've been professional politicians all their lives. My party is particularly guilty about this. If they haven't been professional politicians they've been estate agents or something. Actually they are much more ignorant than the bulk of my colleagues who really have had to survive and work and that's true of the hereditary peers too. I also think we know a lot more about the voluntary side of the Tory Party here. Nearly 70 per cent of all my peers who take my whip in this House, whether hereditary or lifers, have been or are officers of the local Tory Party Association. I don't think that's true of the House of Commons. They know what the Tory Party is thinking out there.

Lord Cranborne, Conservative

If you actually look at the contributions on the floor of the House, it is over-whelmingly the life peers that actually contribute to the day-to-day work of this House. There are a lot of hereditaries that are exceptions but I did actually look at the figures and about 75% of the speeches made are by life peers. So the House could work perfectly adequately if you just got rid of the hereditary peers tomorrow.

Lord Ponsonby, Labour

I'm not a great team man, and if I were asked to join a group of hereditary peers I would shy away. I think we are such a disparate lot. We come from varying backgrounds. You might find a small group of people all of whom had land and who all went to Eton and had been in one of the guards regi-ments. There are small groups like that, but there is no common badge that you can put on them. I think hereditary peers are a very independent lot. I never think about having a title really, except when people become deferen-tial, which they do from time to time, and which is the most off-putting thing about it. The deeper you go in to the provinces, let's say you're asked to do something, to attend some dinner and to make some speech, you might pos-sibly have to enter the chamber or enter the dining room with the mayor and so on. There's a great deal of pomposity and that doesn't really suit me at all. I don't want people to think I am something that I am not, the stereotypical hereditary peer. I still use my ordinary name when I go to the dry cleaners and when I go and book my car in to the garage. In fact I had a great prob-lem once with the gas people here, because we had a boiler which was giving trouble and under our contract they were supposed to come immediately. Well, after two days, and with a small baby, we still hadn't got hot water and we rang up to complain. Finally a very agreeable man came to do the boiler, and he said it was up on their board as Viscount Falkland. And he said, "We're nervous of going to people with titles and that kind of thing, so they get pushed to the end of the queue". I said, "Why's that?" And he said, "It's because management's told us when we go there we've got to put on ties". So I said, "Okay, take me off, I'm plain Mr Carey from now on".

Lord Falkland, Liberal Democrat

I think the hereditary element is a very valuable element indeed, most of all because it mostly comes from outside politics. I came here as a full-time pro-fessor talking about my own business. Which meant that I did know some things about it that other people didn't. And you see this with other people.

The Earl of Littleton who is a chartered surveyor, for example, and Earl Nelson who's a policeman. There are lots of other examples of this. A minister who simply knows the Whitehall brief is no match at all for someone who actually knows what happens on the ground. It's something the Commons doesn't really get enough of.

Lord Russell, Liberal Democrat

There are various kinds of hereditary peers. There are those who never come, those who occasionally come and vote but don't take part in debate, and vote without having listened to the debate and I resent that. There are a significant number who take an active part and whom I wouldn't like to miss. Incidentally, they introduce a younger element in a chamber which, if it was done purely on merit of a lifetime would consist of old people.

Lord Dahrendorf, Liberal Democrat

This House at the moment would find it a bit difficult to function without a few hereditaries to keep the show on the road. You have to have some genuine working life peers, there are lots of them of course and they do very well. A lot of this argument's to do with legitimacy as well as snobbery. A recently ennobled Labour peer stuck his head round the door, as a lot of them do, and said how much he agreed with my line about the House of Lords. Then he said: the truth of the matter Robert is that, if I'm honest with myself, the reason I really love being here is because here am I from a humble background in the same assembly as the Duke of Norfolk and without the Duke of Norfolk I won't enjoy it nearly as much.

On the legitimacy side there's nothing really more legitimate about a life peer than there is about a hereditary peer. The difference between us is that a life peer is nominated by Tony Blair who is still alive, while I was nominated by Queen Elizabeth I or, actually, in my case, my peerage is by James I and I think I have an advantage because at least my patron is dead and can't get at me.

Lord Cranborne, Conservative

I find the speaking rights more significant than the voting ones as I'm not too interested in voting. All the way through what I've done is various things on the side and I'm not a mainstream politician in perhaps the way an MP would have to be. I have all the time, as a peer without main party political commitments, to do all that and didn't Aristotle say, happiness lies in activity. Something of that kind. I have plenty of it here, although if I could no longer sit in the House of Lords, there are other things I could do. It's the speaking rights I value most of all. I don't mind too much about the voting ones.

Lord Sudeley, Conservative

The fact that we're born into a situation is a benefit because we have the training beforehand, we have the expectation. From my own point of view I made sure that I'd have quite a lot of experience in other things before I came in to the House. I have a platform, which very few other people in this country have. But, at the same time, I have a very strong sense of duty. I've been here for nearly 23 years. I think I've done my duty. I've certainly tried to do so. And I've been given the privilege of enjoying all the benefits of being a member of the House of Lords.

Countess of Mar, Cross-bencher

I think hereditary peers come here because they feel a strong sense of responsibility. They have expertise which they readily bring and they use on the floor of the House, but it's the chores of the House, the House Committee, the Officers Committee, and the many other committees that run the House and Select Committees. I just don't think the life peers will give their time freely to do that sort of work. I think the hereditary peers offer so much which is so often not understood by the general public. I think it would be very very difficult to keep the House running, but it's up to this government to say what they want.

Lord Allenby, Cross-bencher

I don't - to put the question right - say hooray for the hereditary element. That's absolutely indefensible and completely daft and in a sane world would be done away with. If all the Commons were prepared to work really hard and do nothing else we wouldn't need a second chamber, we could bring the stuff back again. The party was committed to the abolition of the second chamber, but what was wrong with the plan was that you couldn't have got the Commons to work the stint. They won't work that hard. So there is a case for having time, there is a case for having the civil service come back, to have the pressure groups, there is a case for sending it through another lot of people. The problem with that is that you then run into the whole question of powers, of whether you want to create the second chamber which mirrors the first chamber or whether you want to create a second chamber with the ability to stop the first chamber . All these old problems come so you go round and round with the old issues on how do you get a second chamber - I don't know the answer to that, I couldn't be bothered with all that. I say cut the period of delay and carry on.

Lord McCarthy, Labour

Don't write off somebody because his great, great grandmother was the mistress of the king. Maybe his dad was a dud, but he himself takes it very seriously. I can visualise them now, certain people who are busy, they run companies, they've got jobs, but they do attend. I suppose Cranborne is the best example, because no one can accuse him of not having political nous. Indeed, some people were talking about him as an interim leader of the Conservative Party while it got itself sorted out. What I'm saying is he is someone who is a street-level viscount, if there is such a thing. All I'm saying is don't label people because of their title. Because I can think of one or two life peers who don't turn up much.

Lord Taylor, Conservative

I think some hereditaries make a real contribution. Some of them know a great deal about their specialist area, much of it is in agriculture and that kind of environment, but there are also people who know about other matters, and some of them are very willing to devote themselves here. They go in the chamber and work hard at committee stage, they work on the legislation, they sit on our committees. The Lords Select Committees are very good. You only have to see the difference between what our European Committee produces as a report on agriculture, and the stuff that comes out of the Commons. So they do make a contribution. It wouldn't offend me if a reformed House of Lords left them with the opportunity to elect from among themselves a certain number, or equally that they could be appointed as life peers if they had proved their commitment. But the main problem is that the hereditaries are nearly all Tory. If you start with the basic requirement, which is to eliminate the massive Tory majority, that does mean eliminating a massive lot of Tory hereditaries.

Lord Donoughue, Labour

I don't know quite why people are so much against the idea of heredity. The great thing about heredity it seems to me is that heredity is your mum and dad, and your granny and grandpa and your children and your grandchildren.

151

I think that's very important in this country. Once you start attacking that principle, well you attack the monarchy for one thing. Even worse, you attack the basic principles of civilisation because civilisations are about the family and they are about two people living together in a family and their parents and their children, and possibly uncles and aunts as well. That is what civilisation is built up on. I think to attack that principle is a very bad thing.

Lady Strange, Conservative

As Lloyd George said, like any random body of men plucked from the ranks of the unemployed, they're not all stupid, by any means. But they are of a very limited social background. They don't have any real understanding of life as she is lived. There's a Liberal who's come in having been a detective from the West Yorkshire Police. There are a few odd ones, most come from at most five per cent of society and they're men, with very few exceptions. That's a wrong way to choose people, even if you were choosing people from the ranks of the unemployed. You wouldn't chose them from five per cent of the unemployed and all men. They come and vote. There's an old boy who died recently called the Earl of Orkney. Being half-Scots I asked him what the weather was like in Orkney. He'd lived in Torquay for 15 years until he died recently. Never spoke, voted Conservative in every division, and died full of happiness at the age of 83. An awful lot of them are like that, they really are.

Lord McIntosh, Labour

Of course, it is an anomaly. It's all patronage and I'm not going to defend that because I can't. But the whole thing is an anomaly and you either go for a 100% elected chamber which would cost an awful lot of money, so I don't think that's in anybody's mind, or it's two sets of patronage. It's past in my case, and it's present with life peers. Nobody's been elected. So I don't know how the government is going to change it because the makeup will still be patronage, albeit life peers. Remember quite a lot of them are either past politicians or politicians who have lost their seats and then the others come in from industry and the arts who haven't necessarily in the past played a great part in politics. So you have to think about that form of patronage as well. As our convenor says, if it ain't broke, don't fix it. I think one of the problems would be the enormous cost of an elected chamber and I doubt whether the Commons, in any government and at any time in the future, would be pre-pared to hand over some of its powers to a second elected chamber. If it were elected, you would then have to pay people, and basically, the problem here is no one really gets paid. They get paid expenses, and I do know that my expenses get gobbled up in stamps and taxis.

Lady Wharton, Cross-bencher

The narrow social group, overwhelmingly men, is the weakness. Another is that people are not as directly in contact with people, other than through their families and their work, as the MPs are. Certainly, when I was a local borough councillor, I was much more in touch the issues that were confronting my neighbours and the people I represented in my ward than I am now. It's sad to say that you do sort of drift away from the day-to-day issues that tend to affect most people's lives when you come here, and I think that is a weakness in this House.

Lord Ponsonby, Labour

You could, in principle, appoint more peers. We've got 92 and the Tories have got 494. If you're going to secure a majority, we appoint 400 people. Then you can't work the place. So, you've got to move to a more up-to-date democratic position where the elected government, with a clear mandate, is not facing a massive, permanent Tory majority. If the Tories had got even less in the last election they'd have still had 500 up here. Nothing would have changed. It's a nonsense. Absolute nonsense. So that's to me the reason for changing. I've never minded the hereditary principle at all. But the reason to change is that it's outrageous that a democratically elected, majority government should be treated in here as if it was a small minority that had to be resisted and exhausted.

Lord Donoughue, Labour

It needs reform because it's unbalanced. There is this huge built-in Conservative majority which can't be healthy for democracy. I know it's not a democratic chamber but it's making a contribution to the democratic process and therefore it should be more representative of the balance of power in the other place. Down the years it's been totally out of balance. So I think the hereditary thing has got to go. That's not to say that some of the hereditary peers shouldn't be given life peerages because they will make a contribution. That applies to all sides of the House and to the cross-benchers as well. But there's no logic in it at all. Just because they lent their money or their wives to the king at some stage in the past is no reason for them to be here today.

Lord Tordoff, Liberal Democrat

What you have with people like myself is that broad cross-section of society, different things. You get the dentists, the doctors, medical people, chemists, all kinds of people who have got experience of things that go on in life that you wouldn't normally get in say, a House of Commons, or a House of Lords that's appointed or elected. It throws up a broad cross-section of people who can contribute with specialist knowledge of the work that they do.

Lord Colwyn, Conservative

If one can say as a hereditary peer I have any right to be here, it's simply that my ancestors in the old days were given this hereditary peerage and part of the deal was that their offspring from then on, and their elder sons, were going to be members of the House of Lords. I think in some ways, therefore, I feel that I've got a sort of right to be here, but I don't think I've necessarily got a right to vote. I really do believe we should have voting and non-voting peers. It seems quite a good idea and I think the advantage of hereditary peerage is that you do have odd people who come down with very specialist interest. It adds a sort of element to your second chamber which is non political. You'll think it is political because the hereditary peerage tends to be slightly towards the right I suppose. But you get people with great knowledge and interest, and very interesting people who come and talk about things with authority, which on the whole, politicians don't.

Earl of Glasgow, Liberal Democrat

The hereditary peers add a degree of independence and they also add to the cross-sectional feel. I'd be sad to see them go. But if they do go, I think there must be a proper reform. If you remove those who are appointed merely by patronage you have to decide on what the composition of this House should be. You have to address not only composition but what the House should do and what its relations with another place would be. Why the 1968 programme fell down is the Commons felt threatened that a revived Lords would detract from their power. It's all very difficult.

Lord Henley, Conservative

I'm not really impressed by Labour's start at the moment. It's OK to say you want to change things, but you've got to have something viable to improve the situation before you start talking about changing it. I know that they're saying at the moment they've decided to take away the votes of the hereditary peers, then it could be the thin end of the wedge. It could be a means of getting rid of the whole lot. If they're simply intending to replace it with a second chamber, which is nominated by the Prime Minister, or indeed, the political parties, you're going to get a chamber which is more deferential to the political parties. I think it would actually make things worse. You would-n't get the rebellions that you got on Michael Howard's bill. If you replace it by more nominated peers, I just think there's less chance of independent thought.

Lord Taylor, Conservative

I am, of course, opposed to simply taking away the right of hereditary peers to sit and vote. Apart from anything else, I think the resulting chamber of life peers would be unworkable. I don't think you'd get enough people to come in and do the work on the European Committees and Science and Technology. That's apart from all these private members' bills, and hybrid bills, and all the multifarious activities you have to have from volunteers. I think it would be very difficult to run. You could find yourself in the position of saying, why have it at all? I do believe you can't have this first reform without actually saying what you're going to do. I think one really ought to look both at the Lords and Commons. The Commons has got much too big. Far fewer members, and I would pay them much more, would be better.

I think that the whole lot of legislation needs looking at. These ill-digested bills and vast amounts of clauses and vast amounts of regulations by minis-ters. We do need to get back to really looking at Parliament and that Parliament should act as a check on the executive, that's it's job. It doesn't really do it very well, nowadays under any government.

Lady Young, Conservative

If it's just life peers the chamber won't survive for long because its function will change entirely. At the moment there are so many peers, and because they're spread in different ways, governments can be defeated. A defeat in the Lords at the moment means that it's only sent back to the Commons. They think about it, don't change it one iota, and send it back, and the Lords roll over. I think that's always been the case, except at the end of parliaments where some things can actually change, when you can actually stop govern-ments from doing too much. After the change you're going to have a second chamber which has no power whatsoever. If it becomes a rubber stamp on legislation then I really don't think there's a point to it. It all depends how they do it. Everybody is asking "Are they going to take you out and shoot you?", as if it's suddenly the end of your life. I think it's actually not going to be a very complicated bill. They'll just take away your right not just to vote, but even to attend the House of Lords at all. Parliament is a working building and I don't think you've got the right to come in for a cup of tea if you don't work here. They did it with the Irish peers. It's already happened once, it could happen again.

Lord Redesdale, Liberal Democrat

The only thing that does irritate me is the fact that some hereditary peers either never come here, or, if they do, they don't speak. Hereditary peers come here, and actually ask you, "what's it all about?", and "what's this amendment about?", and "which lobby do I go into?". They're really not interested and I do find that difficult. But I've discussed this with MPs and they say, come off it, Detta, the same happens down our neck of the woods, where people haven't got a clue what they're voting on. They could be voting on two flies going up a wall.

Lady O'Cathain, Conservative

They were always going to be changing the House of Lords, but I think now probably something is actually going to happen, and we're now ready to accept the changes that will occur. As long as the electorate are happy and want the House of Lords to change, I think a lot of the hereditary peers, like myself, will be happy to accept that decision. I have never really been happy accepting the fact that I am a member of the House of Lords and my friend down the road isn't. I think most of us on the hereditary side have accepted that, and we are prepared to move out of the place as long as they put something back in there that's going to do the job as effectively.

Lord Colwyn, Conservative

I think it's absolutely the right thing to do to get rid of the hereditary peers. Hereditary peers are completely indefensible. They tend to come from a very narrow social group, as a whole. They tend to be overwhelmingly Conservative and they also tend to be overwhelmingly men. You can find lots of exceptions to those generalisations but, nevertheless, the generalisations are accurate. For those reasons, apart from the principle of hereditary peerages, it's absolutely right that hereditary peers should go.

Lord Ponsonby, Labour

I can think of just as many life peers who have caused difficulty for the government as hereditary peers but there are two principle arguments for hereditary peers. One is the independence - they owe nothing to anyone, even as to whether they'll turn up here. They are not creatures of patronage. The second is - and you might laugh at this because you say they are all rich, landed and whatever - they reflect a cross-section of the population far more than the life peers who are all people of some distinction or people who've achieved things. The hereditary peers can vary from a very bright, ambitious high achiever, to those who are not very bright and not very ambitious. They are a proper cross-section in a way that all of you in the Commons who've had ambition to push yourself there, and most life peers, are not.

Lord Henley, Conservative

I haven't rebelled while I've been in the House of Lords but I shall rebel if the party is to be seen supporting the eradication of the hereditary peers. I think they have a great value. Firstly because they bring youth and secondly because they only turn up when they're interested, and there is no money of any size to attract them. The sons of these great houses are people who have been brought up in an atmosphere of government, and the ones that take it on are people who have taken it on because of that interest and knowledge. The present leader of the Opposition in the House of Lords, Lord Cranborne, one of the Salisburies, is absolutely worth his weight in gold. His strength and power in terms of being able to make a contribution is because he's a Salisbury, and you couldn't be a Salisbury without being almost forced to do your homework.

Lord Harmar-Nicholls, Conservative

There are two basic objections to reform. What are you going to have in its place? If we have elections, it's going to be rivalry with the House of Commons. If we have a nominated chamber, then it's a Prime Minister's quango, and nobody wants that either. So we should leave it alone. I think it's always been the traditional role of Parliament to curb the executive, and Parliament's very much weakened in that respect, especially the House of Commons use for referenda, guillotines, and the deselection of MPs of course and so forth. It's very important to have in Parliament a hereditary element which is independent. Removal of hereditary peers would remove some of the independence of Parliament which it now possesses to carry out its traditional role of curbing the executive.

Lord Sudeley, Conservative

My God, some of our hereditary peers have worked their socks off. The last government wouldn't have got through in the Lords without the hereditary peers. I'm not talking about the people who came in for the odd vote. I'm talking about the Cranbornes, the Strathclydes, the Henleys. People on the front bench, who give up jobs. I couldn't afford to go on the front bench, because they're paid, what, £35,000 a year or something. You can't do that. If you've been used to a certain standard of living, and if you've got commitments, at a certain level, you can't give them up. This front bench was actually held together by hereditary peers. To throw them out would be crazy because they've got all the experience and the expertise and they're very good, a lot of them. If there has to be reform, I would look at the attendance list, the speaking list and the voting lists, of hereditary peers over the last five years, not in the recent period since the election because everyone was getting scared, so they were attending, and just pick out of these at least 100.

Lady O'Cathain, Conservative

My son will possibly be disappointed. I don't know, I haven't discussed it very much with him. He voted Labour in the last election having taken a considered decision. On the other hand, he's very happy to come in and have a drink and look round the place. I don't think he will mind particularly. He's a very left wing thinker at the moment, but he's 29 years old.

How would you qualify, as a hereditary, to be a life peer? Is it because you're a front bench spokesman, is it because you've done your time? If they do say to each of the political parties you can have a certain number, it's not going to affect Labour or the Liberal Democrats as much, it's going to be very difficult to work out who on the cross-benches is to sit. But there is going to be an enormous amount of fall-out within the Conservative Party. If they say you can have 20 life peers for your hereditary peers and they've got 600, how are they going to choose? It's going to be a bit of bun fight.

Lord Redesdale, Liberal Democrat

What I really think is needed is a House of Lords which is self-confident enough in its position to be able to use the powers it has. At the moment we barely use those powers at all. A lot of people say that that is actually rather a good thing because it makes the system work. With a weak House of Lords it means that there is no gridlock in the legislative process. I actually think that a bit of gridlock would be a good thing because if you put pressure on anybody or any institution they tend to perform better. There's not nearly enough pressure on the House of Commons which performs inadequately. There is only one place where that pressure could actually come and that is the House of Lords.

Lord Cranborne, Conservative

There are only two things you could do with the House. One is that you should keep it roughly as it is but you stop the hereditary peers voting. Or you'd have a certain number of voting peers, maybe a few hereditary peers might be allowed to vote, so voting peers, working peers and just peers. You allow hereditary peers to come if they want to, because every now and again they may be able to contribute something, or make a speech or do something which is quite valuable. I would like to have the opportunity to come down and speak about things that I feel very strongly about and also that I feel that I could contribute to in some way. I don't know why people don't want me to do that. I think that would be quite nice for them to have people like me and other people, but only on issues that I think we could really contribute to. I think quite a lot of them wouldn't bother to come, actually. Presumably, they wouldn't get paid either. I know quite a lot of peers that if they weren't paid their expenses, they wouldn't be able to come. But just getting rid of hereditary peers and leaving a House of Lords of appointed peers is the worst of all possible worlds. I think appointed peers are almost less democratic than hereditary ones. I think there's a certain charm in the House of Lords which will obviously be lost if you get rid of the hereditary peers and it would then be like the House of Commons with a lot more elderly people.

Earl of Glasgow, Liberal Democrat

To abolish hereditaries you'll still have an imbalance of numbers. To even that up you'd have to create some Labour or Liberal life peers and you would end up with more people than you would need to run the House. If that goes on for any length of time before stage two, you've got a House which will be more assertive, albeit all appointed and, therefore, not as legitimate as the House of Commons; more assertive, and more active, and yet the government of the day will not have a majority. So the political and constitutional problems of that will be greater in the limbo period. Even a substantial creation would create some problems.

Tony has said, effectively, what we should do is have a balance in the House of Lords with no single party dominating. I think that's very consen- sually-minded of him, and in some ways, will avoid political flak but actually won't make business here very easy. So I don't think we're going to get a massive creation, we're going to get a creation which evens us up, possibly even slightly exceeds the Tories. Some of the deal will have to be that some of the current hereditaries get translated into life peers including, probably, Cranborne and those elements. But we'd end up with a House of 500 plus. Only 300 play an active part now. If you end up with a House of 500or 600, because you've had to do a balancing act, it's a different beast. It could then think of some more constructive things to do like establishing committees and scrutinising the government. I suspect the government wouldn't be too happy about that but I think that, in the long term, is the role for a second chamber if you need one.

Lord Whitty, Labour

Curiously enough if you change the composition of this House, the whipping would be much more of a problem for the government. The government has said it wants a least a fair majority over the next largest party, and I can understand that. But it has also very sensibly said that it's not going to have an overall majority in the House. This means that it's going to be much more difficult in practical terms for Dennis and Thomas to agree. We sometimes ambush them, but more often than not, it's all done by lots of individual decisions. Theoretically it shouldn't work. Because the Commons are the bosses, and quite right too, we are what Conrad Russell calls the housemaids, "cleaning up". And no more.

Lord Cranborne, Conservative

I introduced a plan which very nearly became law. It would have allowed hereditaries to have come - existing ones anyway - and attend and speak, but not vote. That was accepted by the leaders of two parties. That was the plan. Although I come here every day and hear all the gossip I don't see any other plan to divert a clash between the Houses. The media would love such a clash but a lot of damage would be done to the government. 750 hereditary peers going quietly. Why should they? They'll have a show-down. Mine would be one way of avoiding it. They will be satisfied with just speaking. They will agree to it. If you're a backbencher it's the same old place. Not only a club but a bit of a hospital.

Lord Longford, Labour

CHAPTER NINE

New Labour, New Lords?

LABOUR'S manifesto envisaged a two-stage process of reform. First deal with the hereditaries then make the Lords democratic rather than meritocratic, which the life peers are. Yet to propose any reform at all is to go right to the heart of the perennial peer problem and face the difficulty which has stymied all reform and allowed the Lords to linger on to the end of the 20th Century. Decades of desultory debate have produced no consensus on what form of second chamber Britain should have, what will work or what the Commons will accept. Nor is there any indication that the government or its Cabinet committees on Lords' reform, chaired by the Lord Chancellor, has even begun to think this problem through. Or, indeed, that it will do so unless forced, which a party with a majority of 180 can't be. New Labour's 'third way' is empirical so the government is open to ideas. On this issue there are too many and most are inconvenient.

As a pragmatic party New Labour is also ready to defer problems, and little inclined to stir hornets nests, even if the hornets are old and can't sting very hard. So why bother with substantial reforms when a new government's legislative agenda is long and other problems far more pressing? This is the point at which battle will be joined with those who don't want to embark on the reform train unless they know the ultimate destination of the government; those who are reluctant to enter into the wider, more divisive debate at all; and the cynics who point out that if the wider reform isn't done now, it never will be. The impetus for reform must peter out if postponed to the next parliament and then Labour's majority will be smaller. If the government doesn't do it now when it has a majority big enough to do anything, government is hardly likely to be passionately interested later, particularly if there's no real need for further reform, because a nominated second chamber will almost certainly work, after a fashion, as well as suiting the meritocratic approach of an anti-ideological government. So the hereditaries will go, some with a bang, most with a whimper, all with regrets. They will, however, go more happily if they know something better is to be put in their place. Most don't think it is. As for the wider public, they too prefer a once and for all reform to a long, drawn-out, incomprehensible argument in which everyone is talking on different levels and working from different suppositions.

I'm not in favour of letting sleeping dogs lie. I think this is a subject you can actually do something about once a century. The fact of the matter is that Labour Governments have to scratch around to make sure they get their majorities. You can always put it right down the other end, but what you're really saying is that the British Constitution works providing one of the two chambers of the British constitution doesn't function as it ought to. It seems to me that we've got a real chance now, for the first time certainly since 1910, and probably for even longer than that, to get a rational constitutional settlement between the two Houses. That is worth going for. I know it'll upset people in the House of Commons because whatever you do to the House of Lords, even if you only abolish hereditaries and do nothing else, it will be more troublesome in the future than it has been in the past. Therefore, the Commons has got to get used to the idea that the British Constitution will no longer continue to function on the basis of the reticence of the Upper House.

Lord Richard, Labour

My title is like my pictures. It's part of my history. It's part of what has been handed down like a piece of silver, or any other heirloom really. I don't think my son will be disappointed. I think he realised a long time ago that this wouldn't go on very much longer. So far as reform is concerned, I don't agree with the reform of the House of Lords as the token gesture to reform of Parliament. I think   Parliament needs to be reformed because Parliament has lost its effectiveness, which it needs to have to correct the executive. That is the real reason we need to reform Parliament. The House of Lords may well be part of that to make democracy work better. But I wish that they'd done it in a broader and more comprehensive way. I don't think just reducing the second chamber to appointed or elected peers is necessarily going to do that.

Lord Falkland, Liberal Democrat

Politics is a long game and I suppose I'm in a sense relaxed about it. I've been lucky. I've had an innings nobody could possibly complain about. Life goes on. Curiously, I feel more emotionally involved for my son who'll probably have no interest in politics at all because as a father, although I understand the logic of the debate, you instinctively think , I'd like him to have the opportunity if he wanted to take it, that I had. Simple as that. If I have to go and do something different for the rest of my life, they can't take away from me what I've had and done. I've been very lucky. There's plenty of other things out there to be doing.

Lord Inglewood, Conservative

I will be thrown out of Parliament in the same way as every other hereditary peer will be. I've been assured that I'd be 'reincarnated' as a life peer and I must admit I would welcome that prospect. But given my history and my political viewpoint I think it would be very impressive but very strange if Tony Blair gave me a title.

Lord Monkswell, Labour

I'll regret it going but it's inevitable, I don't look back, I never have. I agree with Douglas Houghton. I remember when I first came into the House and Douglas said to me, "Ziki, don't ever look back. There's always tomorrow". To be honest, I'm sad at going but, in going, I hope I've contributed in some little way to make some animal's life better for having been here. That's the way I look at it. I have made a lot of friends here. I hope I'll be able to keep them.

Lady Wharton, Cross-bencher

I'd be deeply upset if I were superannuated. I was made a life peer to sit in the House of Lords for life. I adore it. I did have this terrible eight years with my husband and being a minister at the same time, and I've never had such kindness. It's like a family. It really is. Dennis Carter, for instance is a very good friend of mine. We used to have fun. Good friends. I've just had a knee replacement operation and I was away from the House for eight weeks, and when I came back, Lord Williams was answering questions, and he said, "I have a quarter of a second left, I would like to welcome Lady Trumpington back into the House." What could be nicer than that? I'd be sad to lose that kind of thing.

Lady Trumpington, Conservative

I would have liked to have seen my daughter in the House of Lords, not that I ever will because I'll be dead by the time she comes into the House of Lords, obviously. But I would have liked her to have had the opportunity. I've given her a little bit of "work experience" in that she worked in the Palace of Westminster for five years before she got married. She is very sensitive to the duty that goes with the title. It saddens me, with such a long line behind me. And many of them have given such excellent service to their country. We've had our black sheep. A few years ago there was a fascist peer who would never attend the House of Lords and refused to attend the Coronation. But that is how families are, there are some good ones and some bad ones - and the good ones shine and the bad ones sink into oblivion.

Countess of Mar, Cross-bencher

I'm not a politician and if I was abolished totally, it wouldn't make that much difference to my life. But I'd definitely miss it and I think the great privilege you have as a hereditary peer is being able to have access to the corridors of power. Very few people have access and that is what you get by being a member. You don't actually have power but you can go and talk to a minister. It gives you a certain advantage. But in general political terms, I don't think anyone's remotely interested in my view.

Earl of Glasgow, Liberal Democrat

The Labour Party has made it a central part of its platform because it needs a bit of red meat to throw to its left wing and its hyped the rhetoric. As it happens I bet the government wishes it'd never started on this path, but it's too late, it's got to do it. Poor Ivor Richard has been proved to be a man too honourable and honest to be a member of this government. Ivor made it very clear that he believed, as I do, in a stronger second chamber and I suspect for exactly the same reasons as I do. He said that in public and no doubt said it in private to the government.

164

Now a stronger second chamber is just what Mr Blair doesn't want because a stronger second chamber would be a chamber that performs it's proper function which is to act as a check on the House of Commons and, therefore, make the House of Commons perform better. Mr Blair doesn't want that. To have a leader of the House of Lords who is promoting a sensible constitutional solution for the second chamber doesn't suit him at all. That confirms my view that Mr Blair has never wanted to proceed to stage two but will stick at stage one as being the easiest thing to accomplish. Which is to abolish the hereditary peerage.

Lord Cranborne, Conservative

The greatest thing that we've got to concentrate on is to remove the right of hereditary peers to sit and vote. No chopping off of heads. A short bill should be passed that says the House of Lords should be restricted to peers of first creation. That is life peers. Not any hereditaries. So that if you're not a life peer, you can't be a member. That means, if you're the Earl of Sandwich, or the Duke of Norfolk, you can continue to call yourself that, but you've got no right to sit and vote. In a democracy, the greatest thing is the vote. So we take that away from them.

If you remove the hereditaries, you're then left with the House which is made up wholly of life peers, all of which have been appointed. The Labour Government is committed to having a second House which is directly elected. So, you've got to move from one thing to the other. I believe we ought to say to people, "we'd like you to tell us what kind of second chamber you want. Whether you want one with regional representation, first past the post, representation from the TUC, the CBI". That is up for grabs and you have a speakers' conference, a Royal Commission. So you have a body which meets and takes evidence and then reports before the end of the five-year term of this parliament on how the second chamber should be elected. I think it ought to be half and half. I think there ought to be a house of 400 with 200 who are elected, 200 who are appointed.

Lord Graham, Labour

It's not a matter of us wishing to indefinitely protect the status quo or defend the hereditary peerage. The hereditary peerage has provided generations of service to this country. But if the time has come for them to go then go they should. But they should be replaced with something equally effective and independent. There are a number of schemes around; from wholly elected

Houses, partly elected Houses, regional lists or representative bodies, for instance, the head of the TUC, or the head of the CBI, and we need to look at all of these things. But I think, given there are so many centrifugal forces at work at the moment within the United Kingdom, we probably ought to find a way of tying those in and acting as an antidote to those centrifugal forces.

Lord Strathclyde, Conservative

You have to decide what you want for a second chamber. The constitutional reformers, from Charter 88 to the Nuffield Foundation, want a second chamber with a legitimacy that comes from a mandate that is different and distinct from that of the Commons. They haven't worked out how, of course.

I don't know of any second chamber in the world that is elected directly. All of the others, if they aren't federal, have mixed systems of appointment or election or whatever. But constitutional reformers want it to have a distinct and independent mandate that comes from election which then acts as a brake on the Commons. Whereas of course, political parties just want to get their business through and they want the Lords to be virtuous in the sense of cleaning up the draughtsmanship. At the end of the day, those two positions are irreconcilable.

Lady Hollis, Labour

Everybody says; we want to reform this House. The hereditary peers are unacceptable in this day and age, and I can't dispute that, but you cannot reform this House in any way and keep its character exactly the same. If you reform the House to get fairness between the parties, you are going to make divisions in the House far more important and ultimately, they will be principally politicians, and as a secondary thing, they will have their outside job or whatever. So you would be altering the character of the House enormously. Now once you get rid of the hereditary peers you will get rid of some of the people who bring in a lot of this expertise. More often than not, life peers are older because they have already achieved some sort of success in life to have caught the eye of people who were choosing them.

One of the things one can do with a life peer list is see whether the House, or your side of the House, is lacking in a particular sort of expertise. I noticed at one moment that there were young, very keen, very well-speaking barristers in the other parties, and we were a bit short. So next time there was a list, I said, for goodness sake, send us some good barristers. I knew there wasn't a vet in either House of Parliament but I discovered there hadn't been a vet in either House this century. So we said, with all these green matters coming up, one must have somebody who can speak authoritatively. We managed to get the best vet we could find. That is a luxury that the new House of Lords will not have.

Lord Denham, Conservative

One of the problems about all this is that, when asked about reforms, they talk largely about composition and not so much about the way we do business and what we do, nor the second stage of reform. What the House of Lords is for is an important constitutional issue which I think we haven't faced up to. Well I hope the Cabinet Committee are facing up to it but I'm not privy to these things. In general discussions it is not being faced up to.

Lord Whitty, Labour

If you're going to have an elected element, the House of Lords has got to have more to do. No one is going to stand up for election for an institution like the House of Lords with its limited powers. After all, it's quite a performance going through an election. It would probably accumulate power if it was elected. But of course then you have got to define very clearly what its power is and what the Commons is going to give up. Certainly if it was an all elected chamber, it would have to have something to say on money matters. After all why, shouldn't they?

One really does need to think very clearly what it is the House of Lords ought to be doing. We have said we are not against reform but we want to see what it is we're really going to have. What we are against is simply removing the right of hereditary peers to sit and vote, without putting anything in its place. That I think is very serious.

Lady Young, Conservative

I think the only way to have a second chamber in our constitution is to have an elected House. I think it's the only democratic way. Life peers are rather better than hereditaries, but not all that much. It's the luck of birth and the luck of the choice. Why have one academic rather than another? I think they have played quite a part and yet I'm afraid some of them take their title and you never see them again. Others come only rarely. I think you probably could have an elected chamber which has lesser powers, and I think the delaying power could be reduced to six months. In these days of rapid communication, I think it's sufficient. The right to reject an order could be dropped, because the problem with orders is, if they're rejected by the Lords, they don't go back to the Commons, they die. As the Lords did with the Rhodesia Order. It had to be reintroduced.

Now the government are beginning to think in terms of 60% elected, and 40% nominated. I think we need some nominated peers because you need your scientists and your doctors and your economists and so on. There's hardly any subject in this chamber on which somebody, including many hereditaries, does not know quite a lot. It's extraordinary.

Lord Strabolgi, Labour

I want two thirds elected and one third nominated. Elected by regional lists, almost certainly on PR. I think that we'd end up then with a totally different type of House from the House of Commons. If you set up an elected Second Chamber with a constituency basis you are asking for trouble, so you don't want to do that. On the other hand I do think that if you have a House of Lords which is two thirds elected, you've got more electoral credibility up here, it actually gives it more weight and authority. The House of Commons may not want it to have more weight and authority but, in the end, it's a healthier house. The ones that are nominated will basically be elitists and cross-benchers. What you should do is phase in the elected with the voluntary retirement of some of the existing life peers. If you add an attendance requirement or something, plus gentle urging that anybody who is over the age of eighty should go, you will gradually get the number of existing life peers down to a level where you could then proceed to the   election. That's not a three month process, you are talking about a matter of a few years. You will then end up with two thirds elected and one third   nominated, and the one third nominated should really be the cross-benchers, the great and the good, that you've got here now. It really doesn't matter what they are called, there is a lot of flummery up here which is frankly nonsense. There is a lot of flummery here and in the Commons and it is immensely difficult to get rid of it. I reformed the introduction ceremony for life peers and there was the most enormous row. It went on for months and months. In the end we got a more sensible and a shorter ceremony but there is still a bit of flummery attached to it. Derry Irvine wants to get rid of the breeches so they don't have to dress up in full court robes. There's a huge row going on over that and I, personally, doubt whether we'll get it through the House. So it's a question of picking the ground to fight on. You won't reform the House of Commons by getting the Sergeant at Arms out of uniform and taking away his sword.

Lord Richard, Labour

People have been discussing reform for over 120 years and nobody's ever found the Holy Grail as to what is the answer to the House of Lords. I think that there is genuinely a feeling around that the time has come for the hereditaries to be replaced by some other system. Fair enough, I make no great opposition to that. What I think is important are two things; first of all to recognise the tremendous work that the hereditary peerage has done in the House of Lords as part of parliament; and, secondly, if we're going to go then we should think very carefully about what is going to replace the hereditary peers. We must not at any cost do what the Labour Government are considering which is to get rid of the hereditaries first and then sit down, scratch their heads, and have a think about what to replace them with. That would be a   terrible thing to do. You would end up with a House that was appointed entirely by the Prime Minister. We'd end up with all kinds of cronyism. It would be a quango House. It would be a House that, by virtue of being appointed entirely by the Prime Minister, would be very much in his grasp

Lord Strathclyde, Conservative

I have canvassed amongst many of the peers here, probably 50 or 60 of the whom I totally respect, and said, "Simple question, if you were to stand election for this place, would you stand?" The answer is always no, I wou n't. I'm not going to stand up in a local hall and say, please vote for me the House of Lords, because I'm great and because I've achieved XY? couldn't do it. And most of the people here couldn't do it. If you had an (tive chamber, you would not retain what you've got here. You would get ple who are self-seeking, who would come for the note paper and the Simple as that.

Lady O'Cathain, Conservat

I would not want to lose the independent mindedness of the members in particular, I would not want to lose the contribution of the cross-ber Because you've got people here who would not come into the p process through a political party. I'm thinking of people from ac from the armed forces for instance, lawyers, business people, trade un people who would simply not put themselves up for election. B nevertheless do make a contribution to the whole process of parliame would not go for a totally elected House. I wouldn't object to some element if necessary on a regional, national basis - Scots, Welsh regions of England. But the problem is not so much here, the proble

the Commons. Once you make this place legitimate, the Commons will take fright. Because once this place becomes legitimate, it'll say, "Hey, we want to do something about money". And the Commons would never allow that. They might be right.

What I'd like to preserve is the ability of this place to fine-tune legislation, to hold a mirror up to the government and the Commons and say, "look you've got this wrong." I think they do that best if we have people up here who are from all walks of life. I don't think you can do that other than through an appointed life peerage frankly.

Lord Tordoff, Liberal Democrat

If you are going for a reformed second chamber by doing it in two steps, and the first step being mere abolition of hereditary peers, it is doomed to disaster. I suspect that the new reformed, appointed-only chamber would still be here 80 years on just like the 1911 Parliament Act says this is merely a temporary act before we bring in total reform. We haven't seen that years later.

Lord Henley, Conservative

I would vote for the first stage to get rid of hereditary peers. But it does worry me that we're going to vote for the first stage and there is no timetable for the second stage. It also worries me that we're actually going to fundamentally change a section of the make up of Parliament without any public debate about the implications. You're going to get rid of hereditary peers, but that changes the nature of the House of Lords. If the House of Lords is no longer the same chamber you have to ask what it does and what is its relationship with the House of Commons. That ultimately leads to "shouldn't you actually look at the whole thing? Shouldn't you reform the whole thing?". That's probably what's going to stop the second stage taking place.

Lord Redesdale, Liberal Democrat

I think the best way is to have a long-term aim of converting the House into a fully nominated element, but while this is going on, pass a short bill to take away the right to sit of inheritors of any sons of the hereditary peerage. It should have been done 30 years ago with these other reforms we were talking about. If it had been done, there would hardly be any hereditary peers here at all. 20 to 25 hereditary peers die every year. So in 30 years the whole lot would have gone except for one or two. At the same time they could then be deciding on the eventual reform. That should have been done after the last

election. God knows if they'd have done it then, by now a year later, we'd have 22 less and by the end of this parliament, we'd have had one hundred less. But they didn't. They go for the whole thing and in the end they might end up in turmoil and trouble.

Lord Strabolgi, Labour

I think there is a very great case for extending the principle of the bishops bench. Senior bishops in the Church of England are ex officio members of the House of Lords. I think the other churches should have the same sort of rights. I see no reason why senior people in commerce and industry, the Trade Union Movement and other professions, by virtue of their senior position in those organisations, should not be ex officio members of the House of Lords. So you could fill it up with expertise from across the country. That would ensure that one had expertise in the House of Lords from different fields.

Lord Monkswell, Labour

There is an argument for the status quo. It's not one I'd buy. I personally think that Parliament would work better if it were balanced a little, with the House of Lords being given more self-confidence by changes made to membership. And I think in itself would do one huge service to the country which would improve the quality of legislation and reduce the amount of it, simply because they wouldn't be able to get as much through. So I do think it needs to change. What I'm against is this stage one reform abolishing the hereditaries without putting anything simultaneously in their place. I personally think that it doesn't particularly matter what the composition is. I'd deplore it if it were too strongly directly elected because it would be a challenge to you lot which causes all sorts of problems. I can't think of anything worse than another lot of professional politicians.

Lord Cranborne, Conservative

I think you have to have a predominantly elected House with an appointed element. Keep the Law Lords, that I would be extremely keen on. Not only for the independence but also because of their value for drafting. Do you remember all the mess that was put right in the bill about recovery of social security benefits after an industrial injury? I remember one of the judges coming down to the House and saying, if this becomes law, I cannot apply it in my court because I have no idea what it means. That's something I'd be very, very reluctant to see us have to give up. The government, which had a secure majority in the Commons, took absolutely no notice of it, and they had to do the whole thing again.

The elective element would be almost all-party. But the importance of the cross-benchers is that they sway the majority in the final vote. So it's like having a jury to talk to. If you're trying to persuade a jury you don't talk in the same way as if you're talking over the other side's head at the other end, and of course you can't do that here anyway because the press gallery's empty. There's never anyone in after 4.30. And if you speak after 11 at night, you're speaking in secret session.

Lord Russell, Liberal Democrat

We have to get rid of any thought that there's going to be a two-stage process in this. In 1911 the big reform was intended to be a first-stage approach to getting something more democratic. 87 years later nothing has happened and we all suspect and believe that this government have no real intention of going on to a stage two. First of all I want to see what all the options are. As part of that I think we should look very carefully at the kind of constitution that is developing in the United Kingdom. We've seen a new parliament for Scotland, an assembly for Wales, new government for London and more power going to Brussels. We need a parliament for the whole of the United Kingdom. I'm not at all convinced that we should go for a wholesale reform until we have seen what kind of United Kingdom we're going to end up with.

Lord Strathclyde, Conservative

I think we should push ahead with the simple reform of the hereditaries, and do that as quickly as possible, despite all the problems it will cause here in terms of the timetable. I think it's probably necessary then to try to establish a consensus on what needs be beyond that. Once the hereditaries have been dealt with, it would be possible to have a cross-party discussion. I think the Tories have been quite clever in the sense of saying, yes, we now accept the abolition of hereditaries in principle, but our commitment is to a more democratic chamber. Therefore they've taken a little bit of a moral ground away from us so we may have to put down a few more markers for principles of the second stage. But actually we won't reach agreement. We could have either some sort of commission looking at it on a cross-party basis. I'm in favour of that process. What I would actually personally like out of it would be a predominantly elected chamber and probably directly elected, by PR. It is difficult to maintain the life peers who currently exist. You'd have to start again. There is an argument for saying abolish life peers the same as we say abolish hereditaries.

Lord Whitty, Labour

In time you need some sort of second chamber but not a more powerful one, like the Senate in the United States. There's no solution everyone can agree on so I think I'd set up a Royal Commission. I wouldn't be in favour of a wholly elected second chamber, abolishing the right of all hereditary peers to speak and vote, because some of them are very good, like Cranborne. He's very good indeed and it will be very difficult, if you have an elected second chamber, to keep people, because they've never been elected by the average voter.

On the whole I prefer a nominated second chamber but you then have to decide on what basis people can be nominated. The services could nominate people for it, we already have the Chief of the General Staff, but I don't see how business could do it because bringing in politics is very hard for business. We shouldn't necessarily call them Lords. I think, for myself, I don't like the title.

Some of the hereditaries are very good. There's that young fellow, Freyberg, he's a solicitor and the grandson of the General, and he's taken the lead in getting better pensions for retired servicemen. There are some who are very able but never come. I've never seen John Julius Norwich at all and I don't think I've ever seen Marcia Falkender.

It's not a perfect second chamber but, then, neither is the Commons a perfect first chamber. It's very desirable to have a second chamber in an advisory role. I don't think it could be elective, the government wouldn't put up with that, and I'd like to keep some of the hereditaries. Get rid of the idiots but some of the best ones on the Tory side are hereditaries.

Lord Healey, Labour

What I do care rather a lot about is that there should continue to be a House with some element of independence of party that can check the executive. That I care about very deeply indeed. I think that means it's got to continue to have cross-benchers. Both for the expertise and for the independence of party, and because they change the way all the rest of us speak. I remember one occasion when Jim Callaghan and a minister were parading insults with each other in pure House of Commons style about their parties' economic records. Oh yes, you did. Oh no, I didn't. And Peter Henderson, the former

Clerk, stood up from the cross-benches and said; what's all this to us. Get back to the question. And they did, very quickly indeed. That's why you've got to have cross-benchers. The other thing is that it does a very great deal to weaken party discipline when you're feeling at loggerheads with your party. There is somewhere else to go and it tremendously alters the balance of power between whips and a dissident member of the party. I've heard of one case recently where somebody was carpeted by his Chief Whip and at the very beginning of the carpeting he said, well if you like, "I'll go and sit on the crossbenches". The carpeting ceased immediately.

Lord Russell, Liberal Democrat

At the end of the day the business is actually run by about 50 people around the House. There are other players; that's probably gone up to about 100. But you are going to have to give quite a lot of life peerages to Tories because most of their peerages have gone as rewards to people who aren't going to roll their sleeves up and be active members. If you are going to expect this not to be a voluntary part-time House, you're going to have to pay it, with all the implications of that. The average age of our people is now in the 70's. They're here until 2 o'clock, 3 o'clock, unpaid.

Lady Hollis, Labour

If you reformed the Lords you would tighten it up and professionalise it. I would certainly draw short of making it a fully professional chamber. You'd have to think very hard before you made it entirely an elected chamber, although there may be a case for regionalising elections. If you'd got a system of regional government in this country you might have secondary nominations from those regional governments, or some other way. As long as you kept the Lords - in terms of its direct mandate - different from and subsidiary to the Commons, then I think you could do lots of things to sharpen it up and make it more effective - but effective in an advisory and a revisory role. As long as you keep the role secondary and supportive, and don't give it ideas above its station then it can do an interesting and effective job, and be an interesting and rewarding place in which to work. I'm very happy in my work.

Lord McNally, Liberal Democrat

What I think is more important is how you get to a consensus. That's my quarrel with the government. I suggested that they should produce a list of options, possibly a Green Paper, and they could have done that last year and not wasted so much time. Anybody knows what they are, we've been discussing it for around 120 years. Then hold hearings in public, try and build a consensus so that at least you've discarded the ones that won't work. Then, when you have a much narrower range of possibilities, mix and match a bit between them. Part-elected, part membership. That's one way I would like. I think it's got quite a good case for it. Then produce a bill with an attempt at consensus. That seems to me a much more sensible way of going about it.

Lord Cranborne, Conservative

I would hope we'd probably get a slightly broader representation from the Church. We are in a multi-cultural, multi-racial, multi-religious society now and I would hope there was some way other representation could come through. I never feel that the Roman Catholics are terribly anxious to get into the Lords but it would be good if there was wider representation. I would hope the kind of representation between 20 and 30 could be sustained only because we are not able to be there all the time. Perhaps it wouldn't be bad thing if we lost six and handed those over the other Churches. One values the contributions of Lord Jakobovits from the Jewish faith and there are, of course, faithful Roman Catholics and Free Church people within the Lords themselves, people like George Thomas and Donald Soper and people like that. I just feel it would improve things.

Bishop of Lincoln

I think that the cross-bench peers are more influential today than they've been for a very long time. One of the reasons is that - this is only my own feeling - a lot of the hereditary peers here are concerned about what might happen to the House of Lords, and on occasions they say so in the chamber, "This is not an issue, my Lords, in which we should put our heads in the noose". I don't think the cross-bench peers feel like that at all. They'll put their head in the noose if they believe it to be right and that's the great strength of them. They take the view that they've nothing to lose.

Lord Weatherill, Cross-bencher

I don't think the hereditaries will resist it in the sense of actually trying to destroy the Bill when it comes. I think they may take quite a long time over amendments and not all directed at improving the Bill. It'll be a tactic of delay rather than anything else. There's not a lot you can do about that, except make people sit up all night, which on the whole, they don't like.

Lord Tordoff, Liberal Democrat

It will be resisted, strongly resisted up here, partly because the Tory leader, Cranborne, is very ideological and reactionary on this. But my view is that we should take that on and as soon as possible. I'd be very surprised if Hague and the new generation of the Tory Shadow Cabinet want to spend next year leading, as their main crusade, the defence of the hereditary principle. Were they to do that, it seems to me to be presenting the new Labour Party with quite a gift. So although it would be fought quite bitterly in the Lords, I would be surprised if the Tory Party wanted that to be their main issue. Hague, I imagine, would be willing to let that reform slip through.

Lord Donoughue, Labour

I don't want the Battle of the Second Chamber. It may blow up in our face and make us extremely unpopular with the public. But I think I may get half way to it. My troops are full of fight. And I hope and believe that Blair now realises that we have the ability to cause serious trouble for him. It would be much more sensible to come to a deal. That deal is not on anything except the transitional arrangements. There needs to be a guarantee that stage two will happen and happen fast. If I can get that, I will be happy. And the hereditaries will go. That's fine. Not a problem.

Lord Cranborne, Conservative

The government must realise that if it goes for a one stage approach with a view, at some point in the future, of going to a stage two and therefore having an interim House, a lot of peers - not just hereditaries but a lot of life peers - would find that deeply objectionable. They would work very hard to frustrate the government's aim. It is a constitutional injustice to provide for an interim House with no guarantee that we are going to a fully reformed House, which is what the Labour party supposedly promised. I think that there are members who feel very strongly that their last duty before being abolished is to make sure they are going to be replaced by something at least as efficient and independent.

Lord Strathclyde, Conservative

Whether reform is delayed depends entirely on whether there's a rump of Tory hereditaries who want to make trouble. The standing orders up here are much looser and more flexible than they are in the Commons and, therefore, you can put out 1000 amendments per bill, all of which would have to go down on the Order Paper, all of which, in theory, can be called. If you've got a dozen or

20 backwoodsmen who can organise who turns up when and does what, then in theory it could be very difficult indeed to take it through. It's not going to be easy to get it through unless the Tories put their hands up and say "We agree". I don't think some of the hereditaries up here are willing to do that. I don't think Hague is looking for a fight. On the other hand, if the government doesn't say at the time when they are introducing the first bill, broadly what they want for the second bill, and give a very clear indication of how you get from stage one to stage two, then I think there could be some trouble up here.

Lord Richard, Labour

I think the hereditary peers will go very quietly. I think the Conservatives are waiting to see what the proposals are going to come up with. Whatever they come up with, it's going to be shot down in flames because people have tried very often in the past. I think there's going to be resistance from any government to having a second chamber that has more power than it does at the moment.

Lord Glasgow, Liberal Democrat

What I adore here is new Old Labour life peers being called "my Lord" by an ex-Coldstream Guard Sergeant Major. They go gooey. It's pure unadulterated bliss. I'm used to the title. To a certain extent it rolls off my back. Ever since I was eight when my grandfather died, people who've been my great-grandfather's keeper, even at that age called me m'Lord which is terribly bad for my character but it did give me time to get used to it earlier. The core of it is it is a part of history, it is part of a duty. I want to see a properly reformed Lords. If it's properly reformed I'll go happy as a sandboy. I'll be sad that my son won't be there and I will miss it obviously, all of those things I accept. But if they do it in the way that's proposed I have every intention of behaving like a football hooligan. Every bill you just put down "Lord Onslow to move the clause do not stay as part of the Bill". Then force a division at the end of every clause, 20 minutes, 270 clauses in a division and you know government business goes into a hole in the wall. Now that's not how Parliament should work but if something is going in there which, in my view, is so fundamentally important as the future of our balanced constitution, I would regard it as my duty to do it.

I don't know if you remember the Queen opening Parliament and saying the hereditary principle has no future in our constitution in the last Labour

Government in '68. It causes gales of mirth all round. It's not beyond the wit of man to set up a Royal Commission with a brief to come up with a new House of Lords, having been told exactly what they want it for. Once you know what it wants to do its powers are easier and actually its composition is not too difficult. It's got to be the upper but junior House without any shadow of doubt at all.

Earl of Onslow, Conservative

We hold them up for one year under the existing scheme. Now if they decide to change the constitution, which they could do, well that's up to them. Basically, they can force a bill through if they so wish by threats and going to the monarch direct. If you abolish the hereditary peers you've got to get rid of all the Royal Family as well. The Duke of York has taken the oath, he can come and speak in the House if he wants to. The Duke of Gloucester has taken the oath. We're not going to go down easily because it's the history and the way of life we've been brought up to. We have responsibility. If we don't fight for it we're giving in too easily.

Lord Allenby, Cross-bencher

I can see a future which would have a hybrid with a proportion elected, a proportion nominated. I think we could actually make a virtue of pluralism. We could say, by the year 2010 we don't know what the British constitution's going to look like. We know what's going to happen to Northern Ireland. We don't know what's going to happen probably to Scotland. We don't know what's going to happen to Wales. Maybe, the safety valve of the system could be this place, in which you could keep re-knitting. Every decade you'll have to knit a different garment, according to the changes. That seems to me a legitimate role that you actually possibly don't want to tie it down too tightly. It's the place where the constitution will grow and develop. Because the Commons cannot change in quite the same way.

Lady Hollis, Labour

I think the hereditary thing is going to go whether I approve or disapprove. The question is, what on earth is this place for? That question hasn't been posed. I'm firmly of the view that as soon as you do anything in this bit of Parliament you're going to affect the other end of the corridor. Because anything you do that gives this place a greater legitimacy is going to lead to changes in the Commons. I don't think they'll like that. Some of the things the House of Commons says and does suggests they're beginning to behave like Charles I in the 1630s. There isn't a divine right in the House of

Commons either. There are two views of your second chamber. Because we're almost in a de facto unicameral system now with a revising and amending chamber you could either remain like that and beef up your revising and amending capacity. Or you can say we want a more genuinely bicameral system - checks and balances.

Go back to the beginning of the last century - pre 1832 - you did have very much a bicameral system. The pressure for democracy grew up, this place responded by shedding its powers and retaining its composition. Therefore it translated itself solely from being a part of a bicameral system to be a revising and amending chamber. What they could have done was to have said, "Yes. We think the bicameral system is an excellent idea. Perhaps we'll change our composition". So you'd have changed the composition here quite radically, but the relationship between the Houses would have remained as it was. I find the possibility of returning to a greater degree of bicameralism attractive because I do think that checks and balances are important. I instinctively favour a greater degree of power coming back here, and it'll have knock-on effects down the corridor.

Lord Inglewood, Conservative

I would press for an elected second chamber because I think if you're going to have a truly representative chamber it should be an elected chamber. There is a full-time role here. One of the great dangers is how you manage to combine people who've got particular experience in one section and probably have a continuing involvement there, with a full-time job. I think the work load here is not so great as to completely exclude continuing to work as a teacher or a doctor or a journalist. An elected chamber would give a better representation, a balance, and more authority.

The bar to it is precisely the authority it would give the second chamber because that would always be a challenge to the Commons and you saw that last time this was mooted. Michael Foot and Enoch Powell combined to make just this point. It's extraordinarily difficult to see, in a single reforming sweep, how you can move to the second chamber for the new Millenium which managed to keep all of the good bits intact. Which is why I think you're going to see reform take place over a long period. There's a fairly transparent attempt at the moment to say "We've got to know how it's going to end up before we take the first step". Well, the British constitution was never developed in that way.

Lord Hollick, Labour

To my mind, the case for reform has been urgent for at least 100 years. That is not a way of saying that I don`t think it`s urgent now. It`s still urgent. It`s one of the great anomalies of the so-called democratic world that we should have this qualification as legislators. The hereditaries are overwhelmingly Conservative so they are a great deal less independent than you or I.

If we are a democracy we should elect the Parliament. That`s where a democracy comes in. The short answer is to get rid of the hereditaries and bring in an elected element, possibly around a half, or may be a bit more, in one move, immediately. The long answer is how should the non-elected element of the new House be composed? There are many arguments about who should be ex officio. I think the Chairman of the CBI and the TUC would be a very good starting point. If that`s too much work for anybody, as well it might be, then both parties should choose their peers at the same time as they choose their new ministers. Let`s call it a senate and they could call themselves senators.

Would I seek election to it? I might. I would certainly want to be in it because I`ve got used to doing that work now and I do enjoy it immensely. The only reason for not wanting to do it would be because I`m a bit old and can`t work quite as hard as I used to. I don`t know whether I would have the energy now to fight an election for it. I`ve got to retire some time.

I don`t think it matters whether or not I`d feel regrets. The place is a manifest injustice and I`d be very happy to have it wholly elected, with one exception. I think there`s one class of peers who ought to remain there and that is the Law Lords.

I have been saying for 40 years that there must be an elected element and that the non-elected element must be much more carefully devised. The codicil to that is that the reform must be in one move because even the tiny minimal reforms of 1968 fell down because of opposition. So I shall be speaking in favour of big bang because it is certain that if we must make it a 100% appointed it would stay like that for decades, possibly for centuries. This is not something I want to bequeath to Britain.

Lord Kennet, Labour

You can`t justify hereditary principles. That is not to say I shan`t be very sorry to cease to be a member and recently my attendance has not been good but I`ve been a minister for 4 years and I shall miss it. What is interesting is what they`re going to do. To remove hereditary peers will, in many ways, be tragic. People like Peter Carrington will be a very serious loss to the nation for his advice. Then you get a House of placemen if you merely have life peers. A House of placemen is, if anything, worse than the hereditary principle. That, I understand, is only to be a temporary stage and in due course - not in the life of this parliament but early in the next one - you will get an elected chamber. Then the problems will start because no House of Commons will want to give any second chamber more power than it's got at the moment, and those are very limited. As a hereditary House it is quite right that they should be so limited, but for an elected House they should have more power. But I don't see the House of Commons of any persuasion granting more powers.

So you come to the problem of where you get people of much work and stature prepared to stand and go through all the bother of electioneering and constituents and all the rest of it, to be a part of a chamber that has got very limited power. I think there will be very real problems. There will be a row if they stick at stage one. I think we'd be quite popular in the country. In recent years, sadly, all our national institutions have come under criticism but the one most vulnerable, the House of Lords, has had surprisingly little. I think it is admired and we do behave sensibly on most occasions. Very often, when we do vote against the government, we represent the feelings of the people. So I think if they don't go through with the final stage of an elected second chamber there will be trouble. I think we are going to make a fight of it. I may go a bit more now in the dying embers of the thing.

When passing the legislation on the present House of Lords, they must make it absolutely clear that they are committed - a firm commitment - to a democratically elected second chamber, elected by proportional representation. For me it's where I'll stand. I was beaten to the House of Commons twice but I would certainly stand for the Lords. It'd be nice to be elected for something. I'm very sorry that it's ending. I agree I haven't been lately but I like to think that I can go occasionally when it interests me. We've been in the Lords a long time and I shall be very sorry. Fortunately, my cousin, Hugh Cavendish, was made a life peer by Margaret Thatcher. So there will be a Cavendish in the new House. That's a great consolation to me, but I'm sorry I shan't be there.

Duke of Devonshire, Cross-bencher

CHAPTER TEN

Ave At Que Vale

THE Lords love their work. It's nicer than the real world and gentler and more charming than the pressured party games along the corridor. Yet the lifestyle they lovingly describe is lived in a protected environment which is being destroyed. The hereditaries have given the House its tone, charm and idiosyncrasy as well as its amateur, part-time ethos of work done out of duty not for reward. Now they go and, like a public school expelling its boarders, the institution will change as the day boys take over.

Unlike every previous Lord's reform this isn't a one-off tinkering to make the unjustifiable more acceptable but a fundamental reform which ends this legislative lifestyle, not with a bang or an exciting rearguard action, but a whimper of "Let me be saved". The hereditaries will be broken, then diluted and after the "Transitional Chamber" everything will go; amateur charm, the humble role as hand polishers of power, and hopefully, the titles. Without the hereditaries there is no basis for their unique combination of deference, coupled with awkwardness; independence coupled with conservatism; ideological apathy coupled with sectarian intransigence; diversity and expertise coupled with amateur idiosyncrasies. With the hairy men succeeded by the smooth men uniqueness is dead in a chamber of less patient, more pushy appointees, who must fit duty into busier lives and will be less ready to do the hack organisational work, the detailed delving, or the mundane roles which keep the place going.

Labour should have thought this through before proposing the abolition of the hereditaries. It didn't. Lingering folk-memories of the way Labour governments had been frustrated by the Lords, and the inferiority complex of opposition sustaining a fear that the same might happen again with a small majority, prompted action. Abolition of the last remaining class enemy offered a nicely radical touch to a manifesto otherwise cautious to the point of conservatism. It looked easy. It was modernising. It wrongfooted the Tories since the hereditary principle is impossible to defend. So no one thought beyond abolition. Whether the Lords were worth tackling early on, and the great difficulties of getting agreement on an alternative, were not considered. The Lords posed no real problem for a government with a huge majority. A confident government with clear priorities could have postponed the issue, even involved the peers in a wider consultation to develop an acceptable alternative. Instead Labour ploughed on. Faced with the possibility of intransigence it resiled from its anti-hereditary principles to retain a tenth of the hereditaries to separate the quick from the dead, and divide opposition. Then it set up a Royal Commission to do the work that the party hadn't bothered with but put it in very safe and predominant conservative hands.

At worst this process could leave Britain with a nominated second chamber and a bigger pool of patronage. In constitutional matters rien ne dure comme le provisoir, as the survival of the Lords themselves proves. At best it means an impotent second chamber evolved by the establishment figures and the status quo men (and two ditto women) of the Royal Commission. Government minds always prefer a weak second chamber taking minor helpful tasks. They prefer control to disturbance and are ready to buy support by patronage, rather than risk a constitutional clash. Yet a pluralistic, lively democracy needs something stronger, livelier and more disruptive.

A second chamber there must be. Britain generates more legislative and governmental work than the smaller democracies with unicameralism, but has fewer legislators per capita than other polities. The legislature chokes up and legislators are overwhelmed by minutiae. Yet there are no easy federal building blocks to give a second chamber a base and a role and few alternative bases apart from direct election which would elect Grade II careerists, and horn lock the two chambers. Particularly if the Second is elected by Proportional Representation.

Back to basics. The Second Chamber should do more than the revision and hand-polishing the Lords had done so well. It should remedy the deficiencies of an overstretched, over-political Commons which can no longer check an executive listening only to the polls and the media rather than the rumpus room of the constitution. The Lords have been the most impressive, but least effective, second chamber in the world. Britain now needs a more powerful chamber to do a real job. Common sense suggests the functions:-

1. Another set of eyes and brains to check legislation and another opportunity to amend. The Commons can't take on more of this but if legislation is kept malleable for longer and more minds are applied to it, the results must be bet-

ter.

2. An opportunity to examine and report on subordinate, delegated legislation which pours out of government and Europe. Little is scrutinised. There is no post-legislative review of such masterpieces as the CSA or the Dangerous Dogs legislation. Parliament rarely hears representations on draft legislation which would involve people and pressure groups at an early stage.

3. Another forum for debate which is neither a Karaoke repetition of the Commons Yah-boo-sucks, or a media fun thing, but an arena for serious discussion, bringing in a wider range of contributions and more experience.

4. Government by Party means that the executive controls the Commons. It must do so for only the people can judge the party and its performance. Yet there should be, elsewhere, a power to check and inconvenience, and to require the executive to think again. The Lords haven't been effective in this role. A new second chamber can be, with a power of delay.

5. Bill, later Lord Blydon, once remarked, "There's a lot of bleeding idiots in the world and they deserve some representation." The Lords has provided some, plus drug dealers, ex-gaol-birds, junkies, lunatics, mystics and paid lobbyists. They should be replaced by a more relevant diversity. A better second chamber needs a wider range of ability than Commons careerists who come in young, malleable and inexperienced and rise through party loyalty. Awkwardness closes doors but grovelling greases hinges. Real debate requires a wider range of backgrounds, experiences and an understanding of the world outside the political game reserve. That can only come from people who won't go through the elective mill.

6. There should of course, still be space for older, more experienced figures. In the Commons age is purged, experience is at a discount, and the political folk memory goes no further back than 1979. While fashions, usually media-generated, have become frenetic, we need a body able to swim, or at least speak, against the tide and take a wider and longer view than a Commons which confronts, and a media which hypes tension. Both are destabilising. The second chamber should lean against such tides, fashions and the executive.

A fully elected second chamber would replicate the party hacks who dominate the first. To build it on Prime Ministerial nomination is ultimately about control and reward. Yet why be tied to any one system of selection? Our vaunted British constitution is really what governments can get away with. So we can make our own rules to suit our purposes and have diverse channels of entry.

Channels of appointment should not be exclusive. An appointed chamber is dependent, its base hardly more legitimate than the hereditary peers, and its sense of duty possibly less, for distinguished appointees are impossibly busy people who are often unable to take on any major role. The dangers are less when life peers are a minority but it becomes more of a problem if it is the only way in because barrels are dredged. Most appointments should be by an independent Public Nominations Panel required to search out individual (not corporate) excellence and the ability to contribute. A minority of political appointments can then be made by party leaders. They do need some patronage.

Half the major states with second chambers have an elective membership. In Britain a wholly elective second chamber would restrict the range of eligibility but a substantial proportion elected by STV from the English regions, Scotland, Wales and Northern Ireland, would provide a new democratic element and a strong voice for more mitigating interests which are all too often ignored in our centralised politics.

Interest group representation is another path. Major unions, professions and such business interests as the CBI and TUC could nominate two representatives each, as well as the Forces, consumers, the voluntary sector and the churches and faiths to replace the bishops. The right should also extend to big metropolitan areas and to the regional and Scottish, Welsh and Northern Ireland Assemblies, once all are a going concern.

The need for experience suggests a minimum age of 40 coupled with a limited tenure of, perhaps, ten years. Neither appointment nor elective terms should coincide with the life of a parliament and the total membership should be larger rather than smaller, to make the second chamber a wide pool of ability, not a full-time job. All this would create a hybrid House with a diverse, experienced membership. They must be well paid, to encourage them to devote a substantial part of their time and talents to Parliament, though keeping their own jobs, activities and roots.

This is not to be a House of Lords by other means. Peerages are the top of the hierarchy the English love so much. The work of the Lords could not have been done without the status and duties of title. But a modern second chamber needs to be an efficient body, not a heraldic fish tank, and should break the link between title and membership. The hereditary and existing life peers will keep their titles but members of the second chamber should not be peers.

Indeed we could replace peerages in future by a British Legion of Honour awarded exclusively for excellence and service, not cash, or even sell titles to pay off the National Debt.

There is no reason why members of the second chamber should have titles as long as they are paid properly to do a serious and dedicated job. Call it's members "Senators", "Elders", "MSCs" (Members of the Second Chamber). "MS" (Members of the Senate), MLCs (Members of the Legislative Council - even "Tribal Elders" or "Honourable" which would certainly distinguish them from the Commons. Title is not important. The many minds which will be applied to devising one will come up with something this side of Ruritania. What is important is a clear and satisfying role, adequately rewarded.

The Lords have played a part in the Great British confidence trick of cloaking power behind a screen of tradition. Yet the central problem of British democracy is not now the threat from the people and mass democracy but the dictatorial power of an executive which controls the legislature, appoints the judiciary and influences, spins and bamboozles the fourth estate and the electorate. Nothing checks its power, except the clamour of the media. The Commons certainly can't, particularly when there is a large majority for the governing party, as there has been for all but nine of the post-war years. That power should be reduced in a consumer democracy where people want the same influence as citizens as they have as consumers. They want to be heard. Denying both produces alienation and angry impotence. The Commons are now less relevant because government listens not to them but the polls and focus groups, and becomes more powerful in the process.

The executive needs a second chamber to scrutinise and improve its legislative output and allow late changes. It can tolerate a second forum of debate as a safety valve. Yet it already has all this in the Lords. The people's purposes are different and Lords reform should concentrate on them by installing checks and balances to put a brake on executive power. The Commons no longer have the power to say "Hold on - think about it". Yet untrammelled power is bad for the character. So a power to get a government to think again must mean an ability to inconvenience and to delay. Both are objectionable if used in partisan fashion, as they have been by a House dominated by Conservative hereditary peers. Yet both would work better with a House which is more representative and legitimate. Indeed, only a legitimate second chamber can be assertive, persuading government to think again and forcing it to explain itself. This would be achieved by a six month delay, plus the power to question and launch motions of censure. All will make for better government, forcing the executive to think things through, explain itself and hesitate before acting. In Britain the worst mistakes have been those where the executive has imposed its will, not those where it has been stopped. The Super Second Chamber will need its own committee system, to remedy the deficiencies of an over-stretched Commons. It will need standing committees to take debates off the floor and several select committees to conduct their own enquiries and supervise policy, preferably by issue rather than department. It could man joint committees with the Commons on rights, open government, Europe and the constitution as well as post-legislative review, two years after passing a law. Pre-legislative enquiry done by committess of the second chamber would allow interest groups and the public to make representations on draft bills thus encouraging people to look to Parliament and to feel involved in it.

The result may not be the best of second chambers nor a "Mother of Second Chambers". There isn't much of the British constitution of which one can truthfully say that. Yet it will be better able to fulfil the roles Britain needs, and be free to develop flexibly as the constitution changes. This will make it a worthy successor to a House of Lords (R.I.P) which has done its best for so long in its endearingly inadequate way.

It may not be a permanent settlement; few second chambers except our House of Lords have survived unchanged for any length of time. Britain's constitution is changing more rapidly than for many decades and a dynamic second chamber will be far better able to adjust with that, catering for new needs and roles as they emerge, an evolving but crucial part of the system. It will also permit us to say "hail and farewell" to the Lords who have served the country so well for so long. They can go into the 'End of the Peers Show', confident in the knowledge that they are making way for something better.

The "Cranborne Compromise"

This proposal to allow a number of hereditary peers to continue to sit in the "interim" House was brokered by Lord Weatherill, Convenor of the Cross-benchers, and agreed between Lord Cranborne and Lady Jay, Leader of the Lords. It was acceptable to the Cabinet as a means of avoiding disruption of the legislative programme and the Reform Bill by last ditch hereditary resistance, but was denounced in the Commons even before it was officially unveiled by William Hague, Conservative Party Leader. He promptly fired Lord Cranborne as Leader in the Lords. So that reform had quickly disposed of the leaders of each political party in the Lords: Lord Richards, Labour Leader, being replaced by the more amenable Baroness Jay, and Lord Cranborne as Tory Leader, as the price of his compromise.

Lord Weatherill describes the development of the proposal:-

There's a book at my office which says "Anybody got any bright ideas about reforming the House of Lords, shove 'em in here". We looked at it from time to time because after the Queen's Speech last year people were pouring in saying what's going to happen about this? Armstrong of Ilminster produced a scheme which provided that hereditary peers should remain to speak and not vote. Then Pearson of Rannoch had a bill which was retaining some of the hereditary peers for a temporary period while Lord Longford, Lord Strabolgi and others were all chatting around the same line, and it seemed that this was a possible approach.

The cross-benchers elected three of us to look after their interest immediately after the last election because it was thought that "reform" might suddenly come and we didn't want to be taken short. The three were the Earl of Carnarvon who was heavily plugged into the hereditaries, Richard Marsh who was a former Labour Cabinet Minister, now a very free spirit on the cross-benches but who had contacts with the Labour Party, and myself as the former Speaker, and previously a Whip, so I've got contacts with the Conservative Party. It was a good team.

We went to see Ivor Richards about this idea. We didn't get terribly far with old Ivor, but it was early days. When we went to see Lady Jay she was very receptive. She was kind enough to invite the three of us to have tea one day to say "Have you got any ideas for us?" The truth of the matter is that there are a few duff chaps here - but a great many hereditaries do a very good job. I've had to appoint people to committees from the cross-benches because we have our proportion and 75% of them are hereditarie. The life peers on the crossbenches are too busy doing operations on people or involved in running a business. They're out in the real world. They don't come in to plod through lobbies and they're certainly not going to come here at 10.30 in the morning to sit on, say, the Statutory Instruments Committee which is very important. So, much of the work on our side is done by hereditaries and if you look at the membership of committees on the Conservative and Liberal benches it would be very largely the same for them. There are some very able hereditary peers in this place.

Then I went to see Robert Cranborne. I have to give him full credit because he took the ball and ran with it and was very largely responsible in the end for getting the whole thing together. He rang me the weekend of the 29th November to say "This thing is going to leak and we must get it off the ground very rapidly". He suggested that we have a press conference the following Wednesday. I said to him, "What's the hurry?" He said, "Well, it's going to leak". So we had this press conference.

We were then asked if we could have it at 3.15 instead of 3 o'clock. When I asked why, the answer was that the government didn't want Tony Blair to have any questions on that day at Question Time and if we had it at 3 o'clock some backbencher might have got hold of it and lobbed a question at him. I was astonished when William Hague himself lobbed one that very afternoon because I thought it had been agreed that this would not happen. That was why our conference was timed for 3.15.

I understand that when Robert Cranborne put the proposition to the Conservative peers he got overwhelming support. Then William Hague sacked him and appointed Thomas Strathclyde who took it only on the basis, as I understand it, that this deal would go forward and that there should be no undue criticism of Robert Cranborne. I just don't believe that Robert would have gone ahead without telling William Hague. What I suspect may have happened is that when he put it to his Shadow Cabinet they said "No" and William Hague then said to Robert, "You've got to pull out of this, it's not party policy" but by then it was too late!

After our press conference a large number of Tory peers came to me saying "Put down your amendment, we'll all vote for it". This had been agreed with the government and it had Cabinet approval. Some of the crossbenchers have taken umbrage at this sharing out between the parties but when you're negotiating you've got to let every party have it's bit of the cake. The important thing was the figures, which are really quite generous. So far as we're concerned, if this goes ahead there'll be 28 cross-benchers who will remain here in this intervening period. When we first started these negotiations I said to myself "I suspect we'll get about 10. Let's play for 15".

When Tony Blair spoke to the cross-bench meeting last year he said he would like to see the independents holding the balance of power. That's been repeated. The Labour manifesto it says that no political party should have a majority in the House of Lords. That means, I judge, that the balance of influence would be held by the independents and this has since been repeated at the despatch box by Lady Jay - we all call her Nice Spice here in this office. So in the future the independents are going to be a very key element in this new chamber.

The role of Parliament is to hold governments to account. I often quote Mr. Gladstone who said to his supporters, "It's not your job to run the country but it's your duty to hold to account those who do". The government is not now being held to account. Nor was Mrs. Thatcher's government held fully to account. That was my concern when I was Speaker - and I confess quite openly that I did my best to ensure that the minority and other unpopular voices got a very fair share of the action. It is the classic role of Speakers to ensure that all views are expressed in Parliament.

Looking back at those days, I remember Neil Kinnock coming to see me shortly after I was elected in '83. It was the second time the Labour Party had been defeated and he was saying "I can't hold them Mr. Speaker, we're going to have to take the struggle elsewhere". I said to him "if you take the struggle elsewhere your party will be unelectable, but much more serious than that you will have destroyed the reputation which we have in our country for keeping our squabbles on the floor of the Chamber". I said "I don't care how tough or rough it's going to be, but that's where it's going to take place and I shall help you where I can to do that". And I did help because it was my duty as the Speaker to look after the rights of minorities when the government had a majority of over 100. This is the situation they've got today down the other end. Today there are some free spirits on the government benches but not enough of them. Furthermore, the opposition is not particularly strong. The only opposition to a very powerful government has been up here in the Lords. It`s very important in terms of checks and balances that governments are held to account.

Yes, I am in favour of reform of the House of Lords. I think we`ve got to start somewhere, but I hope the Royal Commission is going to go on and look at the House of Commons as well because the Commons, in my judgement, needs quite as much reform as the House of Lords. When I was the Speaker I seldom received complaints about bad behaviour but frequently about the empty chamber. I endlessly explained that MPs were present but in their offices dealing with a flood of correspondence. I checked the other day with the Postmaster who confirmed that 40,000 letters come into the Palace of Westminster every day! I think we should curtail this "surgery" business in which we canvas for problems. Many of them should be dealt with by local government representatives. I think you`d get better councillors if they had more authority. I would make the chairmanship and membership of select committees highly prestigious. I would pay the chairmen. I would give them a car, treat them like ministers, make it a job to aspire to because these are the people holding the government to account. The influence of the whips is not so great and party politics is not so evident - indeed reports from select committees are often unanimous.

I think that here in the Lords we should scrap calling ourselves cross-benchers but be independents. I think in future there`s got to be some kind of non party political body, a kind of honours scrutiny committee to appoint independent peers. I believe that the cross-bencher`s role is going to change quite a bit in the future because although today we`ve not been considered working peers we will be in the future. We don`t and should not issue a whip but a notice every week telling our group what`s happening. By definition independents cannot be whipped or told what to do. Cross-benchers are not encouraged to come here just to plod through lobbies - they come in when they think they can make a contribution.

In the last parliament the Conservative Party was frequently defeated. That couldn`t have been done without the votes of the crossbenchers. Similarly in this parliament there have been a number of defeats that wouldn`t have been achieved without the cross-benchers. I can tell you as a matter of absolute fact that if anybody asks me for any advice on what they should do I have to say to them you`d better go into the chamber and listen to the argument! When Robert Cranborne once asked me if we issued a whip I said I wouldn`t think of it. If anybody says have we got a line on this I say you'd better go into the chamber and listen to the argument. "My God!" he said, "you don't do that, do you?" But we do! Powerful speeches here matter much more than in the Commons but we don't hunt as a pack! On the European Elections Bill I tried to stop the rot. Some independents followed me into the government lobby but many more abstained or voted with the opposition. Some said to me afterwards, "I'm afraid we were on a hook". I said, "My God, you were on a hook. You should never have got on it". But I never put them on or take them off hooks. They exercise their individual judgements!

I can't say that the abolition of hereditaries will go smoothly. However I do believe that cross-benchers are getting a very fair deal. Some have come in to say, "You've sold us down the river", to which I reply, "When you're negotiating there comes a point where you've got to say fair enough." I would say that 75% of the cross-benchers think it's fair enough but I can't be certain. However, I have always expressed the view that it is open to any independent cross-bencher to oppose this deal or to amend it. It is an interim measure designed to break a logjam and the indications at the moment are that it will succeed. However, I also tell them that it is open to them to move any amendments they wish such as take out 91 and add 191 or more and see what happens.

Whether the government will take the view that if the House of Lords frustrates legislation the deal is off, that may well be, but I hope that won't arise. I don't think we'll get much disruption on the cross-benches. I'm saying to my friends, a government with a majority has a right to get its business but that has to be balanced against the opposition's equal right to have its say. That's got to be one of the cast iron principles. Years ago when I was made a whip in opposition I remember Willie Whitelaw saying, "Now you're a whip it is your duty to help the government get that business which is in the best interest of our country. We are Her Majesty's loyal opposition". I used to repeat that when I was the Deputy Chief Whip on our side of the House. A government with a majority has got a right to get its business but Her Majesty's loyal opposition should always be constructive rather than destructive!

Let's face it, the "reform" of the Lords was in the government's Manifesto. They've every right to do it. I hope it won't be frustrated but I hope it will be the catalyst for other changes as I've said. In my view, the Commons calls for more urgent reform than the Lords. But in all this we should not overlook the options open to a government with a big majority if the present House of Lords holds up or seeks to frustrate its business. If this was to happen it would be tempting to them in, say, 18 months time to go to the country on a platform of unelected peers v the elected government. I hope this will not happen.

On balance, I think we've got a pretty fair deal. I don't think we would have got more in the negotiations. I didn't think we'd get as many as we've got. That's what politics is all about, everybody has had to give up something but has also got something out of this. The hereditaries have got something, 91 will remain as hereditaries for the interim period. The cross-benchers have got something out of it, 28 of their hereditary peers will stay. The government has got something if its business is not disrupted. I hope that having come to this arrangement we'll all agree to let it go forward. It's a very sensible plan. I'm saying to my friends I believe if this works, as I hope it will work, it's within the bounds of possibility that the Royal Commission may say this has been working well - let's leave it alone. That would preserve continuity and leave in the Lords a number of very able hereditary peers to continue to serve the nation. Surely a consummation devoutly to be wished!

Lord Weatherill, Cross-Bencher

The details of the proposal are set out in the Crossbenchers' statement of 2 December 1998:-

Our Proposal, which we would table as an amendment to the Bill outlines in the Queen's Speech, is as follows:

Both Government and Opposition accept the Government intends to end the right of hereditary peers to sit and vote in the House of Lords.

During the transition to a reformed Upper House, a block of hereditary peers - one tenth of the total - will be elected among its number, and will remain until the transition to stage 2 is complete.

A group of 14 hereditary peers, elected by the whole House, will sit during the transitional phase being available to serve as deputy chairmen and in other capacities in the scrutiny of legislation and the workings of the House.

The Lord Great Chamberlain, as The Queen's representative, and the Earl Marshal, who is responsible for ceremony, would retain their seats until Stage 2 was implemented.

This means that 659 Hereditary peers will immediately lose their right to sit and vote as part of Stage 1, while 91 hereditary peers would remain as part of the transitional House.

It would be understood that the Prime Minister would appoint sufficient Labour peers to achieve parity with the number of peers taking the Tory whip.

We would assume that the normal conventions of the House would apply during the transitional period.

There will be 75 continuing hereditary peers. This is a tenth of the total number of hereditaries, including those on leave of absence and those who belong to no organised group. The 75 will be divided among the four organised groups - Conservative, Labour, Lib Dem and Cross-benchers, in proportion to their overall representation among hereditary peers.

They will thus be divided as follows:

Party	Current Number of Hereditaries	Remaining Number of Hereditaries	Life Peers
Conservative	303	41	214
Labour	18	3	161
Lib Dem	24	3	48
Cross-bench	202	28	148

NB: Excluded from the calculations are 88 "other" hereditary peers who belong to no organised grouping, 68 hereditary peers without a writ of summons and 56 hereditary peers on leave of absence. In addition to the above number of remaining peers there will be 26 Bishops and 9 life peers who belong to no organised grouping.

FAREWELL...